DON'T LOSE YOUR SPARKLE

The Karen Carter Story

A SPECIAL TRIBUTE TO MOLLY

It was Molly's suggestion back in 2016, that I should write my life story. Anyone who knew Molly will testify to her being a caring kind of girl, a girl who did put a lot of thought into other people. She loved life, she was often the life and soul to all the customers at Andrew's Butcher's, in the Market Hall. Many customers remember her with love, they have spoken volumes to me about how lovely she was and how she used to make them laugh. Nobody had one unkind word to say about her.

Molly was my daughter, my third baby, I loved her as much as I loved all my children. Molly will forever remain looking the way she looked on the front cover of this book. Her beautiful nature and her amazing looks shone through. She was nevertheless unaware of how lovely she really was. This picture was taken not long before Molly took her own life and she will always be remembered, not so much for her looks, but for being a wonderfully kind and considerate human being.

Molly, will be also be sadly missed by her grandparents who adored her, her little nephew Harry, who was only three years old at that time, her brother Adam, and partner Olivia and little Ollie, her sisters, Katy and Darcy, her childhood boyfriend and of course, she will always remain in MY heart. Her memory will never fade. Molly lives on through us all and the people who miss her most.

 RIP to our sweet hearted girl.

5

LIFE ON THE ESTATE

I was brought up on an estate in a working-class area. Throughout my life I have loved reading books. As a child in the 1980s I was becoming quite a rebel and was easily led. To start with we started sniffing glue and shoplifting. For this I was always grounded and I deserved to be. I disliked school I only enjoyed learning English and doing Art. At an early age I was infatuated with fire. I remember mum and dad talking in the kitchen after coming in from work after a long day. For whatever reason I still don't know why I stuck a sheet of newspaper in the fire and threw it into the waste-paper bin in the lounge (It was a metal bin)

I was terrified when the contents of the bin shot up in flames. All I could do was shout out loud. *'The bin's on fire'*. Dad came running in and threw the bin outside in the garden. As you might imagine my mum and dad were more than angry with me.

I vividly remember my dad chasing upstairs behind me and grabbing onto the back pocket of the jeans I was wearing. I had managed to get free which left my dad holding on to the pocket which had torn off. I know I shouldn't laugh about it, because to be honest it really wasn't funny. Dad was strict with me and never made threats without carrying them out so I was never let off and rightly so! I received a severe telling off and a smack and I still don't know why I did it? As a punishment I was grounded. My mum and dad worked hard in factories full time. I was left on my own to get up to all sorts. Although I had my Nana living close by if I needed to go around to her house but generally I would spend time outside during the holiday.

As an only child I was surrounded by friends from all walks of life I could never see the bad in people. They say you live and learn, in my case I learned the hard way.

Several of the kids on the estate got hold of a tin of evo-stick so we decided to try sniffing it. We put it inside a carrier bag and inhaled it. I didn't realise the dangers of this and really it is a dreadful phase of my life.

One day I decided to give shoplifting a go and I do admit I was feeling reasonable brave as I went into the shop in town called Woolworth. Egged on by the older ones I went in and stole a tin of glue to sniff, which we had, later on at a local beauty spot named Healey Heights. I expect I also wanted to prove something to the others but I must admit I felt nervous and scared.

As I rushed out of the store I must have drawn attention to myself as the store detective made a dash to grab hold of me. I ran like the clappers and was way too fast for him to catch me.

It seemed I was destined to be a rebel as I always had to go that extra mile. When everyone else had stopped sniffing glue I carried on. This resulted in me collapsing and waking up in hospital because I had completely blacked out. There were so many things we had got up to and we always seemed to find a way to get hold of money. Many times having been given money by our parents for cookery ingredients we hadn't gone into school at all. We just walked into town and spent it.

It was around this time I remember, around the age of eleven years old something more serious happened. It was during the summer holidays. I spent a great deal of time outdoors as both my parents worked Monday to Friday and apart from going to see my Nana there was a lot of time spent with my friends. It wasn't unusual that kids were left on their own during school holidays as most of the kids I knew had working parents as well. We had to find ways to make our own fun during the 1970/80s.

However, one day during the holidays my friend Emily and I decided to buy a box of matches. At the back of our houses were some garages. We walked around there and found an abandoned car. As we struck match after match the car set alight, then there was an enormous fire ball erupted into the air followed by an explosive boom! Fire was quickly spreading towards other adjacent garages so I ran as quickly as I could to the nearest telephone box. Shaking and feeling frightened to death I picked up the receiver and dialled 999 and reported the fire to the emergency services.

All the kids from the area were gathered around as the fire engine arrived at the same time as the police. It was after the fire had been extinguished that the police started talking to all the kids who were hanging around watching the fire to find out if they knew anything about it. Before he got around to speaking to me though, I made a quick exit and headed home.

On arriving back to my home I looked at mum who appeared to be angry and looked in a bad mood. All her washing had been hanging out in the back garden and the black smoke from the fire had landed black smutty marks all over her clean washing.

'Who on earth is lighting a fire during the day?' she stormed.

It was at this point I was feeling extremely nervous.

Knock. Knock. My mother's front door had a frosted glass panel down the centre and I could see clearly the shadow of a policeman's hat. My breath almost stopped as I knew for certain what was coming next.

My mum went absolutely ballistic once the policeman explained that someone had seen us setting the abandoned car alight and they had been given mine and my friend Emily's name.

As quickly as you can say pyromaniac my fire lighting days were once and forever over. On this occasion my punishment was to be grounded for six weeks during the school holidays.

To be honest I was never a girly girl, I loved being outside in the open air we had a lot of countryside around our house to explore. Close-by where we lived we had many country lanes and small rivers. I could spend hours building dams with my friends across the small stream and tying ropes to the trees, swinging backwards and forwards. So many activities we invented and enjoyed like making secret dens. I often returned home muddied up to my eyes.

Outdoor games like hide and seek or rounders or many different ball games, kids spent many hours outside, back in the day. It's seems sad to think not many kids are enjoying the outdoor life as we did, although I'm not advocating they follow in my footsteps regarding the types of scrapes I got into. It wouldn't do them any harm to start spending time outdoors away from their Xboxes or mobile phone, which is all they seem to enjoy doing now.

I've always had a love of music as well as my other love of truanting from school as I've already mentioned I was a bit of a wild child to say the least. Still I had a lot of friends and back in the day you would play out all day without a care.

Today it's worrying for any young girls who are being groomed and taken advantage of, being given mobile phones and bottles of vodka and then introduced to drugs. Then to be told it was payback time and would be told they then had to prostitute themselves, to whomever the groomers decided they should sleep with. Of course money is received by them to carrying on grooming others young innocent girls. Although I expect it may have happened, I was not aware of this happening in Burnley in the 80s.

Don't ask me why but I stole some straw from a pet shop and this is the time I was caught and had a free ride in a police car. Once again my parents were extremely upset and angry with me. Somehow my mother didn't ever see the funny side of stealing straw whereas my friends thought it was hilarious and took the Mickey out of me for months. After being grounded once more I was also put on report at school so that was the turning point for me.

After this incident a plan was formulated over a thirteen week period. I would have to be signed in on an ID card which was recorded by the teacher and signed by my parents to prove I was in school.

The game was up! I was miserable at school, partly because I'd missed so much time truanting and messing up my life.

The 1980s era was a great time to grow up. Listening to a range of music like Rick Astley, who I wouldn't be caught dead listening to it today, sorry Rick but Bob Marley took over at this time when people were enjoying their first puff of cannabis, which I may add wasn't for me. Then along came *UB40* when drinking alcohol was part of growing up but for me the music was all I needed at this time drink did nothing for me. My most favourite music it has to be said was *The Stone Roses.* I never cease to get bored of them. In 1983 Manchester born Ian

Brown of the *Roses* still sends a shiver down my spine when I hear the album playing

I was totally happy as a kid escaping from the classroom environment, before the confusion of adult life and the harsh reality of life took hold.

I just never seem to settle into school life always longing to be outside in the woodlands nearby the council estate where I lived. Everyone knew each other and if they didn't, someone they knew, knew more about you than you did, hilarious. Those who live on an estate will understand this.

I'll give you an example of this. One day I was sheltering in a phone box with a few pals and my mum comes running down street, grabs me by scruff of neck drags me home saying

'You've been seen sniffing something I saw you with your head inside your coat'

So then she began the body search, finding a big fat nothing. Much to her surprise I explained I had been blowing warm air down my sleeve to keep my hands warm. So then she explained she had received a phone call off an anonymous caller saying I was sniffing glue under my coat. So there you go, just for once I was not up to anything!

During this time a friend and I, babysat for a few kids on the estate somewhere warm to hang out. Myself and Wendy who are still good friends today would play cards a watch MTV. The person I baby sat for was the only person who had the luxury of this music channel. I could sit for hours watching it. We also made popcorn in a clear Pyrex pan and had many mishaps with making it popping all over the place. So, with a packet of Players Black cigarettes and money for sweets what more could I want.

NO MORE TRUANTING

After changing schools and attending my senior school I felt lost and unhappy so once again drifted back into truanting. I spent many hours at the library. The main reason being it was warm and more importantly I loved reading. I do regret missing so much schooling as I'm an avid reader yet I have to admit I do struggle with punctuation and grammar. I read loads and loads of books many written by Steven King.

Well, here I go again somehow I always seem to get caught. I was making my way through to the library when I bumped smack into my dad who looked as shocked as I did. My brain went into overdrive as I quickly made up a story and explained to him that I'd been sent there from school to do some research on a book. I'm not sure whether he believed me or not but then the school got in touch with him to let him know I was truanting and he was not pleased with me at all so I was grounded.

It wasn't that I disliked school it was the fact that I was so far behind in my work. I truly regret it now and I am so thankful that my own children have worked hard and never missed school. They have impeccable manners and so attentive at school they enjoyed it and always happy to go to school.

However, slowly but surely I realised I had to change my ways so I made a determined effort to attend school on a more permanent basis.

I have to admit I did look forward to the English and Art lesson. I found the art class exciting and was eager to go to lessons. It was interesting with many different things to experience like making clay cups or ceramic tiles and decorating them. I enjoyed painting and learning the many aspects of painting too and found it totally absorbing.

When some of my art work was displayed on the wall in the art room I was thrilled. I liked my art teacher, in fact, I think he was the best teacher as far as I was concerned and the only person who took an interest in my work and always praised me when I did good work. He taught me to try many different forms of art and encouraged me to put more effort into my painting and not waste this valuable time of learning and I will always be thankful to him because he helped me to settle down a little more in classes.

I suppose it was love at first sight when we met. Nicky lived over back from my friend Wendy's house and we soon became inseparable going everywhere together. I thought the world of him and then he ran away and next thing I know he's put inside a place for bad lads called Redbank. He sometimes used to check out of Redbank and arrive home for the weekend but dreaded turning up on his mother's doorstep.

I expect the family were informed when Nicky went AWOL from the centre and would have expected him to walk through the door. Obviously, I was his first port of call; he told me he was unable to go home as he had big problems with his mum and his sister. His mother and sister would take the dog Blackie out to search for Nicky. He was so frighten to return home because he was scared that his mother would smack him one for being absent from Redbank.

Sadly, Nicky owned up to being involved in drug taking and started drinking alcohol and we just drifted apart and eventually lost touch, strange how young love has to go through heartache with all the ups and downs that life it brings. As I'm writing this now and looking back, I sigh, you never forget your first love but I have remained friends with his big sister who is lovely as is her partner Sam.

Many years later I cried for week when I found out Nicky had passed away. Wendy, my good friend and I, both attended his funeral it was a very sad time. He died of a drug overdose he was only 40 years old. Damn you drugs! I can't abide it! People who sell this filth should rot in hell truly devastating for families and friends, when tragically kids die as a result of years of taking drugs it's such a painful useless loss of life.

Rest in peace Nicky, shine bright. I still have some memories of the happy days and still see you in my mind's eye. You walking up road along with two nuns and you had been fully dressed in nun's robes, as. I think the nuns were helping to soften the blow when you arrived home. It still brings tears of happiness to my eyes, everyone loved you Nicky you could be so hilariously funny it's good to be able to laugh. We shared the same kind of music of U2 an UB40 happy times better memories.

Eventually the day arrived and I left school aged sixteen. My first job was to do casual work at a factory and it was great for a few weeks. Many of my friends were on a Youth Training Scheme only earning £30 a week, slave labour in my opinion. At that time I was more than happy to earn twice that amount, yet it didn't last long though and I was laid off. In the eighties you could leave one job and begin another a week later

My first real employment was at a factory called Fenton Packaging, where I was packing cake boards. I started work at 7am and worked until 5pm. The building no longer exists today it's been demolished. The job entailed packing boxes as I mentioned. At first I couldn't keep up the boxes kept flying past me and everyone was laughing. However, I finally got the hang of it and it became much easier for me and the money was good. The lighting however was dim there being only a skylight window in the roof and to be honest I rarely looked up from the job to see the light. Although I was earning good money it was back breaking work.

I hadn't been working there very long when I saw the sun streaming through the skylight I know it was madness but seeing as it was my dinner break I made my way outside. It was a glorious sunny afternoon and it felt good as I walked along down by the canal. However along the way I bumped into some of my old friends. John was there and a few others so I strolled along with them without a care in the world. Needless to say I did not go back into work for the rest of the day.

I knew John back in the day, he was someone who I liked a lot and we had a lot of laughs together. He was twenty at that time and I was fourteen years. I suppose I must have always been on the lookout for excitement in my life and sadly there are many times I did get it wrong.

My family banned me from seeing him because of his age and the fact he had been in and out of prison for petty crime. However, one day when we were on the canal bank he decided to break the padlock on one of the long boats which was moored up. We stood there laughing as it drifted away down the canal. Again I knew I was getting in too deep yet in the moment I could only think that it was harmless fun I suppose. I thought it's only a broken padlock. I never seem to look at the bigger picture. Of course it would have been dangerous as it floated on without anyone on board. All I could think about is the fun we had going along the canal bank getting into all kinds of scrapes.

It was shortly after this prank I decided it was about time I grew up and it was time to take stock of my life and start to sort myself out once and for all. John was not a person whose company I should be seeking.

Because of skiving off work and meeting up with him that sunny afternoon cost me my job, I was instantly sacked.

I didn't dare tell my dad and for a while I pretended to set off at the normal time to make it appear I was going to work. I kept this up for about a week but finally had to own up and tell him the truth. He was not happy with me but insisted on getting me up early every day to go down to the job centre.

Sadly, many years later I heard John got into drugs and methadone (a heroin substitute) and had ended up homeless and had been living rough on the streets. He was found dead in a doorway in the middle of winter. It was sad news to hear as I always will remember the fun times we spent together and I do have some good memories of John. I always try to think the best of people and never condemn anyone they always have their own agenda and it's not for me to judge. Sadly he chose to take his own life.

Looking back now I realise he wasn't the best person to be involved with but I take things as they come and to me we just had a little fun travelling another path in his short life. Seems my life is forming a pattern by meeting lads who somehow turned into drug addicts. This seems to be the type of life I'm drifting into. I must obviously be attracted to danger and seem destined to go down the wrong side of the track.

My next employment was at The Christmas Factory on Leyland Road in Burnley. I worked Saturday and Sunday doing overtime and I loved the people and the banter and soon began going out to the pub. I have never enjoyed drinking and do not drink a lot of alcohol to the present day I feel that binge drinking only makes people ill. I certainly met some colourful people there in this place of work. Again this building has also been demolished over time.

This was where I met my friend Wendy at this well-known catalogue company back in the day. In fact, we started employment on the same day and I began going out with Wendy at the weekends. To be honest though I was just as happy to go home and watch cartoons on the TV during the week. This work, however, was a temporary job and only lasted over the Christmas period.

YOUNG, FOOLISH AND DESPERATE TIMES

It was around this time I met up with a lad I knew from school days at a night club and I started going out with him. It didn't take long before I became pregnant in 1990 and still a teenager. I gave birth to my little girl Katie a healthy and a lovely baby. Yet again my choice of partner is not exactly the kind you would want to introduce to your parents. Why is it I'm always drawn to the wrong type of boyfriend? He had already served time in prison and a regular jail bird, constantly being sent down for burglary and that type of petty crime. To be honest he spent most of his youth at Her Majesty's Service. Due to the circumstances, after the birth of Katie, we took up residence with my mum and dad for a while in their home.

It wasn't easy being on my own with a small child to look after and it was also hard for my parents, so I made the decision it was about time I should move on with my young child and take responsibility. I realised life wouldn't be easy but needed to make plans. So I decided to do a house share with a friend of mine but I was soon to find out my friend was a bit of a nightmare to live with. She liked to sleep around with Asian men and all sorts of people were coming and going at the house. It was becoming clear to me that I couldn't bring my child up in this environment and so I went down to the Council Offices and put my name down on the list for a council house which I hoped wouldn't take too long.

I needed to start acting responsibly and to start to take control of my life, settled down and begin to take life more seriously. I owed it to Katie and I was determined to do the best I could to give her As good as a life as I could. I filled out application forms down at the council offices and requested a house transfer. I was secretly hoping I might be eligible to get the house which had become vacated right next door to my mum's house. My health visitor was exceptionally helpful as she wrote a note to the council which I hoped would help me get a transfer as quickly as possible.

It must have done the trick because not long after I received a phone call to say that I would be re-housed and to my great surprise it turned out to be the house I had hoped for, the one right next door to my mums! I was ecstatic and danced up and down with excitement, I was over the moon. The new house did, indeed, need a lot of work doing to it and the garden was overgrown like a jungle out there but I didn't care one bit. For the first time in a long time I was happy and practically skipped to bed at night I felt free at last!

I think also because I had my daughter Katie to look after it may have helped my case. From time to time I wrote to her dad who was still serving time in prison. He suggested that perhaps we could meet up once he was released. Sadly on release from prison he started to show his true colours. He accused me of cheating on him. He called me all kinds of names and if I so much as looked at another guy he went ballistic. He regularly head butted me for absolutely no reason at all. There is no excuse as to why he turned so violent because as far as I was aware he never drank alcohol and as far as I knew he wasn't taking any uncontrolled drugs.

Now I had my own home it became another issue for him to throw out about and he often ended up creating a row. He kept saying he didn't feel like the house was his own. Well, it wasn't his; it was my house in my name.

He never ever apologised for his terrible behaviour or told me he was sorry. At the time I felt extremely vulnerable and was almost convinced he would end up killing me, he was so violent.

I know after all that I've said when he finally asked me to marry him, I can't explain why I did that, but I agreed. How I wish I could have turned the clock back. We married two years after we met and he was actually on the run from prison. Why did the alarm bells not ring in my head I don't know I must have been totally crazy but at the time I was young and he could turn on the charm when he wanted to. I fathomed in some far-fetched way he would change and settle down with me and Katie.

As the months passed by and when Peter wasn't actually incarcerated in a prison he did get a job and things seemed to settle down for a while. Money was always in short supply and although we struggled we always seemed to keep our heads above water. However, it was never long before he would be picked up again for some robbery or something and ended up being locked up again.

My Nana was my best friend and special to me and when she was diagnosed with cancer I was devastated. I used to see my Nana every day and I was so sad when she didn't even live long enough to see my son, Adam. Yes! I was pregnant with my second child and I was heartbroken not to have my Nana with me any longer.

Nana played a large part of my life from being a young child I would spend a lot of time at her home during the holidays, while my mum and dad worked. We went on holiday abroad as well, which is why I always loved the idea of travelling to different countries. Yet little did I know at this time how this word reverberates in my mind today.

As I grew up I would call in everyday on my way to the shops to see my Nana and she would come to my house all the time. My Granddad was a quiet man, my Nana being the talker. Every Christmas we would all gather at my mum and dads for Christmas dinner. Nothing to me seems the same since my Nana died. I've never been a big fan of Christmas, if I'm honest. I do always have many happy memories of this wonderful lady and I'll always have those special moment we spent together stored in my heart.

My mother was with me when I gave birth to my son, Adam. She had also been holding my hand giving her support when I give birth to my first child, Katie.

Whilst Peter was serving time in prison it became hard for me to pay for things and sadly, I had to resort to stealing baby food and other items from Kwik Save. It seems amazing that I never got caught as I must have looked guilty at the time, I couldn't have lied to save my life, yet somehow no-one ever stopped me. We once ate bacon for a full week as I used to swap labels around in the freezer cabinets. I'm not proud of myself but I was struggling hard to pay the essential gas and electricity bills and never wanted to ask anyone for financial help.

Just two days after my son was born my husband, Peter was released from prison it was then that things changed for the worst.

Day after day he beat me, my life became a misery. One day not long after that he forced me to have sex with him despite the fact I'd had to have stitches following the birth of Adam. He continued to brutally attack me and on one occasion at the top of the stairs he head-butting me in the face breaking my nose. I had to go to hospital for treatment and was in there for hours.

23

During my marriage a lot of awful things took place I was constantly accused of various things I had never done and he had brow beaten me all the time. I dare not even look up at him. On one occasion, I'd asked him for ten pounds, I was beaten. The physical pain was nothing compared to the mental torture I was facing on a daily basis. I don't think this type of torment ever leaves you, it runs there at the back of your mind like a stagnant river of despair.

The continuing trauma of him turning up at all hours of the night still stays with me. I did go to court to get an injunction against him to stop him from abusing me but he never took any notice of that and played the game all night long.

When the police came he would hide somewhere close-by and when they left the house he would return. I often lay awake waiting for the knock at the door. I barely ever slept and it has left me traumatized and I suffered from sleep deprivation.

Nothing will eradicate this from my mind, my nose is still crooked to remind me of his brutal treatment. I was meant to go back for an operation but at the time I couldn't face the pain and today it's hardly noticeable until I point it out to people and they always ask me why had I married someone like this.

It's always wiser after the event I suppose, but to be honest he wasn't always this bad towards me in the early days. What's that saying to me? *We live and we learn*? It would be easier with hindsight I suppose we can all sit there and wonder why?

Many times he would leave and then before long he was back again in my front garden tapping on the window and telling me how sorry he was and could he come back. I would end up feeling sorry for him and so I gave him a second, third and maybe a fourth chance to change his ways, he never did.

It was never long before he would lay down the law and start treating me terribly again. I was obviously very naïve and a trusting person and also a caring person (I still am today it's in my nature). Yet somehow I craved for things to be good again and to some extent I possibly still cared about him at that time, as daft as that sounds.

The very next offensive and terrible thing he did to me took place soon after his return from yet another jail sentence. He locked me in the house and told me he had killed someone. I sat there rigid with fear awaiting my fate and tried to mentally prepare myself for death. I honestly thought that this was it!

I watched him as he stripped off all his blooded clothes and even his leather belt and put them all in the washing machine. Sitting still and feeling numb with fear I felt truly petrified he had the door keys, I couldn't get out. This went on for hours and hours until the morning light began to creep through the window. Only then did he admit to me that he'd been lying about killing someone. I mean, what kind of person behaves like that? How could he conjure up such behaviour and put fear into someone's mind to control me like that? It was without doubt mental cruelty to do that, surely? Christ! He must have been more than a touch mad!

Another time he said he went to the shop to buy an onion and didn't return for a week. I'd thought that this had been very strange behaviour, indeed.

I somehow must have dug myself into a deep hole of despair I felt unable to do anything to get out of this nightmare. I had two children to look after at that time and a jail bird of a father who mistreated me and I also had the children to look after despite that he had continually done nothing but cause us all pain.

He would buy his daughter a gift and then take it back off her. I mean. What kind of a dad does this sort of thing to his own flesh and blood? He also took the living room carpet away because he had paid for it. As if that wasn't bad enough he turned up in a black cab taxi another time and proceeded to dig out sections of the fence at the front of my house and load it into the cab and drive off.

Lots of my belongings came and went I used to get upset and cry but after a while it stopped hurting I became immune to all his stupid unnecessary antics.

He cheated on me regularly with known drug users, which of course, was a big worry for me. I decided to get myself checked out and went to the doctor.

Whilst it had been degrading for me to have to confront the fact that the bastard may have infected me with AIDS, a very serious condition, I needed to reassure myself I was healthy. I often asked myself. What the fuck did I do to deserve this? I thank God I was clear.

I asked myself this question many times. Why the hell are you putting up with this? I started to sleep with a knife under my pillow my nerves by this time were in tatters.

The nights were long and seemed to last forever. Some people wish they could be young again, I, honestly never have, they were possibly the worst years for me. If it hadn't been for my children I don't think I would have coped, yet somehow I found the strength from somewhere to battle on for the kids, I loved so much, they kept me going, although during these times, although I'd felt the loneliest person on earth.

In the early days I would fight back. What chance did I have against someone like him? I feared for my life many times I ran to safety in the early hours of morning wearing no shoes, the police would go and collect the children and take them to my mum's house while I was getting fixed up at hospital.

I would sit in the waiting room with a towel over my face so no one would talk to me my head was full of lumps and my hair had been pulled out in clumps it hurt so much to brush it that I just kept crying all the time when I saw myself.

My family, as you may be wondering, were to say the least, fuming seeing how bruised and scarred I looked and how much pain I'd been in, which only added to my stress having to see me in such a stat, to be honest. My dad actually chased him around the house with a hammer, which ended up with the bedroom window being smashed out. I don't know to this day what went on in that room.

I constantly lived in fear of him and there were so many times I had to run from my home in the middle of the night with Katie, holding her hand and clinging on tightly to my baby, Adam to my chest to escape him. I used to end up at my Nana's house where I knew we would be safe. How I miss her love and kindness. She would never turn us away.

Since Adam had been born, I had still had to suffer the abuse yet had to carry on, I'd still had to flee the house, many times. On another occasion, I ran out of the house to phone the police from a call box, because he'd cut the phone wire at home. I reported to the police he had acid in the fridge then on another occasion I reported there was stolen property in the house. I'd go home and wait and wait for the police to arrive but they never did.

So now not only was he a nightmare to live with he'd now got into drug dealing. He was selling acid, also known as (LSD) or trips. He stored these in our fridge in our home.

One night he decided we would go out to a nightclub; this was a big mistake as he told me all night long to stop looking at men. It's incredulous to expect me not to look at people dancing in a night club but I most certainly wasn't trying to flirt or show any interest in the opposite sex.

After leaving the nightclub that evening he dragged me out of the taxi by my hair, head butted me and hung me on the wooden fence. Unable to move, hanging here by my jumper I felt like Jesus Christ with blood running down my face. Needless to say I was hospitalised once more. I was obviously, totally in fear of him. I was never allowed to have friends. He had full control of me, I was a total wreck by now.

Clearly he was not right in the head yet appeared a nice friendly guy when others were around us.

It didn't take him long to be returned to jail. Night after night I hardly ever slept due to all the trauma I'd been through. I was so affected by all that I'd gone through. I did try so many times to get rid of him, but he wouldn't leave us alone.

On one occasion he broke into the house and had put a gun to my head and clicked the catch. To have to live like this would put fear in anyone, for sure. I was terrified. After begging me to let him see the kids I relented. Later that same day I had to pick the children up from the police station, he'd burgled a house and left them outside it!

You'd think enough is enough yet again he smashed his way into the house destroying everything, I mean everything, windows, doors, carpets torn up, more upsetting he smashed the picture I had of my Nana in a frame, my lovely Nana. I hated him. My daughter Katie had started nursery at this time, thankfully Adam was still a young baby and slept a lot, I was relieved about that

So on and on it went, more charges, he was always caught. Once I woke up to find the house was full of stolen property. My young daughter Katie used to think he fixed televisions.

The days approaching Christmas was like an advent calendar to me as it was the run up to the Crown Court date. I knew it would be a long sentence - I hoped!

During the court hearing they were reading out the charges, many of them I knew nothing about. How long a sentence I kept thinking I couldn't add them up quickly enough. The probation officer informed me he'd been given a twenty-eight month sentence. Once they'd led him away I made my way below the court room to see him. it was then I'd made the decision to tell him that I'd had enough and finally at last I'd found the courage to tell him it was over for good. As soon as I could I filed for a divorce.

Returning home from court, I had a long leisurely bath and actually slept a full solid night. I could hardly contain my inner most emotions I felt euphoric, yet unable to actually believe I was free at last. The door was finally locked and for me this chapter of my life was truly over.

I hated the bastard with a passion. Yet he still tried to terrify me for a number of years by sending me threatening letters, he even arranged for two girls to attack me and beat me up. Then he would tantalize me with other types of written threats like '*its countdown day, one more day to go'… etc.*'

At that moment in time though I had felt bad but it hadn't lasted forever. I'd begun to have faith in myself, I'd grown up, I'd needed to, for myself and my kids. I'd had the time to recover and look at what he'd done to me and possibly scarred my children's mines. He'd controlled my life for way too long, At last I'd taken hold of my life and had finally found the strength to do something about it. I've since learned not to rely on no-one, The children needed protecting and it was my responsibility to give them some stability in their young lives. There had been no other choice, I'd made up my mind to move away from that life, I owed it to me and the children.

OUT OF THE FRYING PAN INTO THE FIRE

Thank goodness I'm still alive and since finally ridding myself of my abusive husband and the bad experiences in my life. I have moved on and I have begun to enjoy the simple things of sitting, quietly indoors reading or sometimes just enjoying walking out in the country in silence, for hours and thinking of nothing. I enjoyed the peace too much, sometimes. I'd think to myself if I ever get rich I'll live on a desert island with a few good books in perfect peace with myself and the world.

Sadly it appears that for me things don't last forever and as my life goes forward there are other things which seem to stop me from enjoying the simple life, I'd always craved. Yet, where there is a need I will always be there for my children and my family, which unfolds as the years go by.

I did get jobs around this time although it was cash in hand. I was able to give the children a good Christmas yet I missed my Nana terribly she had been such a force in my life and at this time of year especially.

When push comes to shove you are capable of anything and everything where your children are involved even when they are older they are still a big part of your life and somehow you manage to cope and get through.

Mentally, I was not in a good place I was lacking a good night's sleep with having to feed the baby in the night and also care for my three-year=old daughter and having to work to keep us all.

The one thing I've always made a point of telling everyone is, never to take illegal drugs. The day had arrived however, when my life was getting out of control and my usual coping mechanism had finally given up on me. I'd felt at that moment I had no choice I had to find a way to keep going, the only thing I knew about to boost my energy was the drug 'speed'. I hoped for a time it would help me to get through each day without me going under or having a nervous breakdown.

My first experience began when having a night out with a friend, Rachel who lived further down the road from me. She had told me that 'speed' would help me to cope. She said it gives you a good night and you still feel wide awake and you don't feel groggy or feel drunk.

I took it for a year and have to admit I was my own worst enemy, although it had helped me get through each day, it had also helped me to forget all the dreadful traumas I'd suffered. I'd known that I was on a downward slope. The only thing stopping me from going under altogether was the love I had for my children. It seemed to me there was never any offer of help or counselling available to me during this time, it's not an excuse for what I did but it is a reason for why I did it.

Soon after experimenting I became addicted to it and had to pay £10 a wrap off a man who lived nearby. Taking this drug however, does make you lose your appetite and what I didn't spend on food I spent on 'speed'

I began to work as a stand-in cleaner for Burnley Borough Council as I needed to feed and clothe and care of my two young children. The only way I could cope with the life and stress of my life was to continue taking speed, it gave me the energy to get me through. I still lacked sleep and the hours of back breaking cleaning was beginning taking a lot out of me as well as suffering from the lack of sleep deprecation.

Due to the drugs I was on I began to lose a lot of weight and felt sick all the time. It was then I finally decided to come off the *speed*. I have never taken the drug since and these days I'm still don't advocate anyone takes drugs. I have seen what it does to people first hand, and without a doubt it does ruins lives. I have lost a few friends due to being involved in taking drugs. It's not a good habit to get into at all, it only brings grief. It's also awful when you stop this despicable habit, which is extremely hard to kick, I was lucky to get help to get off the drug before it took my life. This white vile powder is unbelievably additive and an awful substance to ever get involved with.

Around this time I had a brief affair with someone even though I knew that I wasn't ready for a new relationship. I became pregnant with my daughter, Molly that was when I decided to turned my life around and I immediately cut all contact with him. Molly, is a delightful child, we all loved her dearly except when she screams blue murder at nights. I swear she could break glass it was that loud, but she was loved by us all.

I remember being skint and counting out two pence coins for bread at Christmas. I bought toys from a catalogue (my friends nicknamed me catalogue Karen). It had taken me a year to pay off the debt, and then I would start again for a further year being in debt.

I hadn't realised how much effect this had on me to be honest, I do remember crying when I opened a gas bill and could not even remember ever feeling the warmth of the heating in the house, it always felt cold to me. It's only now I could actually face eating corned beef or minced beef, because that's all we lived on for a long time. It had taken me a year to get off the drugs and I found music became important to me and helped to block out all the bad thoughts.

During my darkest days I became ill and visited the doctors on a weekly basis for my medication, I don't know what got me through these periods of deep depression, if I'm honest, I felt so alone. I couldn't speak or face anyone, at all. I'd just spent hours, simply existing, living in silence. Even my love of books and music hadn't seemed to have worked. Life had been too hard for me. Everything had got on top of me. Without sleeping pills and anti-depressant drugs I don't think I would have slept at all. It was only because of taking these prescribed drugs that I was completely knocked out. I found a certain amount of restfulness and peace, yet some days I'm surprised that I even woke up at all.

At some point the medicines had helped me to rest my brain, slowly but surely I began to start feeling better and I started to get back on track.

A TIME OF CHANGE

My young children were doing well at school I was still working and enjoying listening to music and reading in my spare time. I love travelling, though not so much the flying or having to wait around an airport. Yet I loved trying the cuisine of foreign places and, of course, the sunshine and beaches.

I planned and organised a holiday to Bulgaria with the kids. It was good for all of us, we'd enjoyed the warmth of the sun, walking or having a swim in the pool we'd loved it as a family, it was good for me to see my children happy. I'd been proud of myself having found a way to do this my spiriting away a little money every week to fund this.

I think my Nana must have given me the taste for travel, or maybe it's a case of once I'd been abroad, I wanted more. For me it's a luxury I can't really afford and yet it had been important to me to make it happen, When I'm determined, I'm strong and made it happen. I'd worked hard all year didn't have any social life, never went outside the house, I didn't drink alcohol or gone to bingo or anything. Somehow, I'd managed to save every single penny I could. We had never starved, but I was extremely careful with money, never spending any more than I had needed to, just so I could take my kids away to a sunny climate once a year.

Travel really had to be part of our lives, it was in my blood, like a desperate need, and there had been no stopping me finding a way to afford it, and I'd made it happen.

As my children grew older I still could not fight off the anxiety, it took all my strength to be a one parent family. My oldest daughter Katie was going through problems of her own and had left home. It broke my heart.

No doubt about it my first marriage had left its mark on me. Years of not sleeping and what I gone through. I was taking prescribed sleeping pills called Zopiclone, once more, and advised to take it for a week. I felt numb and was walking around like a zombie.

It was then I decided to take action with my life. I made myself an action plan. Set my alarm for six in the morning and walked for miles. I also pledged to only eat healthy food and after a while I lost weight and began to feel more confident.

Then the awful nightmare with the Social Security Office began, I'd been considered unwell and in no fit state to work due to my depressed state of mind. I had presented sick notes every fortnight that I was totally unfit to work. The doctor had no problem in signing my sick notes he knew full well that I was physically and mentally exhausted, unable to work.

I was informed I was to attend a medical on a Saturday morning. I was in such a low mood it only put me in fear and exacerbated my state of mind. I felt as if I was living through a dream as I was totally numb, I sat in the waiting room alone for well over an hour awaiting my fate.

My name was called and I went in front of a panel of people who made me feel judged and degraded, all I ever wanted was to feel well and go out to work.

All the questions they asked me did not equate to my condition. Could I make a phone call? Could I lift a pencil? How did I get to the medical? How did I wash? I was not saying I couldn't wash or ring people the Questions went on for a while which made me feel more and more upset it made me want to cry in frustration. In fact, I know I did cry at one point.

The minute I left the medical, I returned home and I continued to live on in my medicated zombie life. Mental health is not something that goes away, I was unable to pull myself together and I could not see a way forward to get myself out of the cycle of life and be well and able to cope.

Then I developed my brown envelope panic attacks and had a hatred for the mail to arrive through the letter box. To this the day, I have a dread, in respect of the *brown envelope syndrome*? Receiving a brown envelope is always a sign of bad news to me.

My insides churned in anticipation as I believe everyone who's been through the medical assessment would understand. A week had passed and finally my brown envelope arrived. As a rule if I received brown envelopes on a Friday I chose not to open them for fear of sinking into a complete mental breakdown state throughout that weekend. So, I filed them, which means I threw them in a dark place where they stayed until Monday morning.

The dreaded brown envelope opening day always arrives and need to be opened that sick feeling in the pit of my stomach didn't leave me as I read it and read it again. I couldn't take in what it told me that – *I WAS FIT FOR WORK!* It was there in front of my eyes, it appeared that the amount of points awarded to me at the recent medical assessment meeting had been, eleven. It would have needed to be fifteen to pass their stringent ruling. I cried for a good hour slumped against my front door. I never felt so low in my life I wanted to be well I honestly did.

I rang The Citizen Advice they were really nice and explained that I could appeal against the decision made. A man called Paul helped me through filling out my appeal form. When I say form, I mean more like ten forms then he gave me a Welfare Number. Truly without the help of these kind people who work at the Citizens Advise I would never have known I had rights and would certainly have gone over the edge without their help.

THE CALM BEFORE THE STORM

A few years later on I met someone who changed my life. He encouraged me to be my own person. After suffering years of being controlled by my ex-husband I'd found that my new partner was the opposite as he'd encouraged me to go out and for once I could choose my own clothes and have money of my own, (something which had never happened during my relationship with my ex-husband) for the first time in a long while I'd felt calm. These were the happy times. We'd all taken a holiday to Tenerife together (my children and his son from a previous relationship). Sadly, this idyllic period didn't last long. He'd begun to take drugs and we ended up in debt. We argued a lot and this put a strain on our relationship.

However, in the meantime I'd realised I was pregnant with my fourth child and no matter what, I knew one way or another we would get through, as I always had done in the past. Abortion, to me, was never an option, I loved children and this child would be as loved as their siblings are.

Little did I know then there was another cloud on the arisen which was something none of us could have predicted.

My lovely mum became ill. She began to have dizzy spells and passing out. My dad made a few trips with her to hospital but they kept sending her home with tablets to take. It was awful to see her looking so ill. I wasn't totally equipped to a lot with expecting my daughter at the time and still working.

Finally the doctor did a home visit and seeing how critically ill she looked he immediately called an ambulance.

She was admitted straight away as we followed the ambulance by car. After being sent for scans and having

39

several tests carried out, mum started vomiting and looked terribly ill. I was terribly scared and all of us were extremely upset and worried. Once the results were known she was immediately transferred to Preston hospital as it was serious.

We finally learned that mum had a large brain tumour. We were all devastated by the diagnosis I was crying uncontrollably. It was a worrying time for all of us. We would travel daily backwards and forwards to Preston hospital, we'd be there from early evening, arriving back home in the dark. Mum was put on a course of steroids to see if these would shrink the tumour before a major operation to remove it. My dad had to sign the form to say it was okay to go ahead. Mum, as you can imagine was emotional. Not only because of the forthcoming operation but the fact she may have to lose her hair. Mum had and still has beautiful hair.

After the operation was over mum started to put on loads of weight, this was due to the steroids which apparently give you a large appetite to build yourself back up. At was a lovely hospital the staff was caring and supportive and helpful. My mum was eating well, so much so, even though she is a small lady she was eating enough food for ten people.

Once the operation had taken place and the biopsy test resulted in, our family and my mum having to face the fact, it was a cancerous tumour. The following treatment was for mum to undergo radiotherapy. She was extremely upset about this treatment as she had to wear a face mask and had to be strapped down on the radiotherapy table, a particularly brutal and frightening experience for her.

You would imagine thing couldn't get any worse, yet it did, not long after the radiotherapy mum found out she had lung cancer. It was terrible news for all of us. What doesn't kill you makes you stronger, I suppose. Mum had to face more stress and treatments this had been the worst year of her life.

Life is full of surprises as it turned out, even the medical staff and the doctors were amazed by mum's recovery and it was wonderful that mum was finally after months of treatments and convalescence she was considered to be well enough to go back to work. I would like to think it helped enormously with us always being such a caring and close-knit family unit and very supportive in every way to help mum through the worst days. We are so close, in other ways in that I do live next door to my mum and dad. This had to be a miracle, that although she had to suffer for a full year, we had been so relieved and blessed to have mum back with us.

What a welcome addition it had been once my darling Darcy was born. This is something which lifted our spirits she was a beautiful distraction from all the awful suffering and trauma we had all gone through with mum being so ill. Darcy brought love and joy to us all as all my children had.

It always makes me laugh when I think about the wig my mother brought and wore. It was bloody terrible she looked like Blanch off Coronation Street. (Sorry Blanch) We laughed so much but for once they were tears of joy and a little bit of relief I think. But I have to tell you mum never wore it again, we laugh about this even today.

MY BOY BECOMES A SOLDIER

I suppose I was another low point in my life and it didn't help me cope any better when my son announced he was going to make enquiries about joining the army. I was taking antidepressants once again. I had been diagnosed with Post Traumatic Stress Disorder.

As the time got closer to my son leaving school he started to make plans and contacted the army to see about a career with them. He received a reply and was asked to attend an interview where he had to fill in forms even though he wasn't old enough to leave school at that point. However, as soon as he reached the age of sixteen years old, he immediately applied again as he had been advised he would be able to join then.

I remember packing him on to the train to Edinburgh where he was to undergo medicals and selection before he could be accepted for army life. I had bought him a suit and he sent me a text message to inform me the officer in charge wanted to know if his mum knew he was joining up, because the suit drowned him. That amused us all. We kept in touch by text messages and he told me he was enjoying the initiation selection. He was accepted and offered a place at Harrogate but not until he was able to officially leave school at the end of term when he would be sixteen years old.

Myself and the girls met Adam off the train when he arrived back from Edinburgh. We all went out for a pub meal to celebrate we felt so proud of him and enjoyed catching up with all what he had been up to whilst in Edinburgh.

Wanting to get used to looking out for himself Adam started learning domestic things such as ironing his own clothes. With three girls in the house this was a chore Adam never had to do.

I missed him a lot and had cried a lot, until I'd got used to him being away. The army did not allow any contact for six weeks Monday to Friday but we looked forward to seeing him on the weekends when he was allowed to come home. We had plenty of time to catch up then and he told us he was finding it hard with army life and having to be up and out of bed early dressed and ready and out. One morning he had overslept and all his clothes had been thrown out of window at the camp. This is what they do when someone misses being on parade dressed and ready and with their squads.

Whilst doing his preliminary training he went to see many war graves and also had time out skiing but this didn't last too long. He came home on occasion and brought new friends he'd made in the forces with him along with bags of muddy washing. He looked and sounded totally committed to the army and enjoying his training immensely.

Finally after twelve months training, he was dressed in all the regalia at the passing out parade. We were all very proud of him and my parents and me and his two sisters arrived in style to watch this, his special day. We wanted to look at our best on the day so myself and his older sister Katie decided to have a spray tan for the occasion (mistake). Unfortunately the tan was very much darker than we had anticipated; we both looked as though we'd been on holiday in Africa for a month. Adam told us later he had no trouble spotting us as we stood out from the crowd with our over the top tans. We laughed a lot about that but the day was his and we all enjoyed being there supporting him.

Once we returned back home we had a party with family members and friends. My mind was a little in turmoil at the time as I knew that my son was now a fully fledge soldier and would possibly be sent to war torn countries like Afghanistan, but I tried my best not to let him see I was feeling sad and did my best to get into the party mood and enjoyed whatever time we had together if only for a short time.

When he returned to his camp he moved on to join his regiment The Scots Guards in London at Wellington Barracks where he was on guard duty for a few months at Buckingham Palace. This was a very special and prestigious honour and one I felt so proud of him. He wasn't able to get home so much now as it was expensive to travel from London up to home but we always kept in touch with text messages and the Face book page. He even spent his birthday that year without us but his friends bought a great big balloon, a card and a cake so it made his day enjoyable.

Not long after he arrived in London they began to practice for the yearly Changing of the Guard at Buckingham Palace and luckily Adam managed to get us tickets to go and watch. Unfortunately, my circumstances at the time made it impossible to afford for us all to go and see him so we had to settle for watching it on TV. The camera at one point zoomed in and there he was 'my Adam' right at the front. My heart turned a somersault he looked amazing. Myself and all the family were enthralled and so proud of our lad, we all had a lump in our throats and tears in our eyes, how proud we had all felt of Adam..

After this Adam was posted to Canada on exercises for three months. By now I was getting used to him being away but thanks to Face book and text message we were always in touch and seeing him on a regular basis kept my spirits up.

Once he was back home from Canada we had a big get together him when he returned back home to us, we had decided to do a welcome home party just for him together with a few drinks to celebrate. It never seemed that long before he's off again and then the dreaded posting arrived.

Adam and his regiment would to be going out to serve in Afghanistan. Before he left, my dad had driven us all down to the Catterick Barracks for a family day and to see him before he went on tour. Nothing ever goes the way you want it though. Dad had forgotten the sat-nav and the journey down there became fraught as he kept getting lost. Plus the fact there had been constant telling offs from my mum. It had all quite hilarious, Darcy, and I just kept sniggering in the back seat. However, we finally arrived in one piece and finally pulled in at our destination.

Firstly, we were given a tour around the artillery and given all the information about what our lads would be doing and the tanks they may be driving. It was hard to believe what Adam would be facing and I started to feel shaky when faced with the intensity of it all. We took a memorable picture of little Darcy standing close to one of the tanks knowing at that any time soon Adam would soon be on the way to war.

A few weeks later it was time for us all to say goodbye to Adam. There wasn't a dry eye in the house as one by one of us took the phone off each other to speak to him. It's not as it he was going away on holiday this time he was on his way to fight for his country and a proud day for him. It was so hard for us all speaking to him as we all sobbed into the phone. So much so the phone was steamed up by the time we had all finished saying our goodbyes to him. There was only Adam who managed to keep a wobble out of his voice but then again they are brought up to be tough soldiers who are expected not to show their emotions.

For myself it was an awful period waiting, wondering, worrying, crying the not knowing gets to you day on day. It's hard not to think the worst especially when you hear a soldier has been shot in Afghanistan and his body is being shipped back home. It sounds terrible but the need to look on Face book trying to find out information and feeling relieved, yet sad, for the other guy if it's not your son that got the bullet. I cried all the time and that Christmas it was very cold and miserable here in the North West and we felt the chill of not having our loved one at home with us. None of us felt we could enjoy the festive season whilst Adam, my son, their brother, their grandson was in the middle of turmoil and fighting.

THE BROWN ENVELOPE SYNDROME

The brown envelopes kept on coming and I was trying to survive on forty pounds a week with bills mounting up. These brown envelopes were often left in my dark place and stayed there for a very long while.

It had taken twelve months for me to get a Welfare Number. Truly without the help of these kind people who work at the Citizens Advise Bureau, I don't know I would never have known what to do and I know I would surely have gone over the edge without their help.

The lady from the Welfare Rights was an absolute angel she came and met me and supported me as we entered the waiting area for the appeal. She squeezed my hand and gave me a kindly hug and we sat there watching the sign to see when we were able to go through to the meeting.

I was really heavily medicated so it was all a bit hazy. They asked me questions on how I was surviving they had my medical records they asked what I was doing to help myself. I was having intense therapy sessions three times a week, taking my medication which had horrible side effects. I hadn't smoke cigarettes for over a year I just had no money for such luxury. After being questioned we were asked to go back to the waiting area for five minutes. I felt so under the weather that when we were recalled back into the room I honestly could not comprehend a word of what they had said. Ushering me back into a side room my helping angel threw her arms around me and gave me an

'Karen, you won your case.'

It was not what I was expecting all I was fighting for was to feel well again. This time lapse had hindered my health terribly. I've since read about people who have committed suicide due to the way they have been treated during their medical assessments.

It was explained to me that the monies would be backdated and I would then be able to get up-to date with all my overdue bills and be free of debts. However, it took 13 weeks for this to happen. When I looked at the amount they had paid me I almost fainted. I immediately went and paid all of my bills and sorted through the letters that had mounted up and then I spent as much as I could on tinned food and jars and pre-packed goods and made up a large food parcel and posted it off to Adam who was serving in the forces in Afghanistan.

I felt overjoyed being able to send off as many food boxes as I could over the coming weeks for Adam to share with Scott, one of his buddies. The Christmas boxes we made up included, Christmas hats, together with spam, chilly, flapjacks, crisps, and cups of soup, and anything which would remind them of home. I think I probably sent around 40 boxes of food over a period of three months. I was never away from the Post Office. I think I was probably in that post office more than the Post Master!

For a long while I did still suffer from nightmares and sleep deprivation it seemed the only thing that helped me was the sound of music. *The Street's stay positive* to Stone Roses - *Crank up the Music* helped to get me through, I felt in a safe place. I didn't socialize much as I when I listened to people moaning about their problems, which to them may have been a problem, I would think *'Please is that all you have to worry about?'* In a way I must have been strong enough to go it alone on my journey in life.

After my three months of therapy I decided that I had to come off the medication and I spent two weeks terribly poorly. The sleeping tablet I was on was only intended to be taken for a week yet I needed to take them Zopiclone for seven months. I felt utterly terrible and decided to change my life for the better. I began getting up very early and walking for miles as I thought this would help me to sleep normally without taking medication. It worked and so I continued to do this over a long period of time, in fact, I often go for six-mile walks even today and feel so much better. I never believed I could set myself such a challenge and succeed.

Until you go through these bad times in your life and have suffered in the way I had and yet managed to return to normal I find it hard to compare my life now with that of a very dear friend who died of a heroin overdose during this time. Rest in peace my dear friend.

I bear no grudges, the past is the past, I had to move on and let go of all the anger.

To try to describe my life before now, it was a merely existence. I was in a black hole. In a rut with no way out, I needed the medication at that time in my life but, I'm glad I no longer need it. I have a lot of time for people suffering in this same way. Keep strong, Karen, people would say think positively. It's easy to be told that, now when I look back to these times, it makes me realize how truly lucky I am today.

I continued to work and this time I was working legitimately. I was in the system as a self-employed cleaner, I felt so proud of myself. Nothing ever seems to be straight forward for me as I found out I was in trouble with my council tax which would mean we would be eviction from our home.

Fortunately an ex councillor sorted all the paperwork out for me and got me the help I needed to get the eviction squashed.

I met a lovely lady called Tracy who works and still does, at Calico who now rent out the majority of properties in Burnley. She is one amazing lady I used to meet her in town. They say when special people come into your life they come for a reason. I then decided to join my local Spiritual Church where I became a regular visitor. I'd sit there quietly listening to the mediums. I loved it. I also went to the circle on a Wednesday where I met a lady called Janet who is older than me and had her own problems yet she always had time to speak to me and ask how I was. I felt so grateful to these people.

I was beginning to make many friends another of these is Sarah who has also been through rehab and we have been together throughout the awful years and she is such a caring and loving person who my youngest daughter Darcy, adores. I was still regularly listening to my music Oasis *I want a good life (*a private joke between Sarah and I). We spoke many times about going to Canada, France, never Afghanistan! I would not want to go there.

I was drawn to the Spiritual Church around this time I felt unable to cope with paying bills and being the bread winner. I felt extremely worn down with nowhere to turn. I was having problems over my council tax among other problems. I have carried on since then by attending the church on a regular basis for well over two years now. On occasions I help Kevin at the spiritual church to make the tea. I instantly felt at peace when I walked in there, it is where I met many lovely people. I often go along with Sarah, a particular friend of mine, but even if Sarah is unable to come I still feel perfectly at home there as soon as I walk in on my alone, they always welcome me with open arms.

Whenever I enter this church I feel total calm and at peace with the world. I have changed so much for the better and feel no bitterness towards anyone or anything. I now enjoy taking walks listening to my music and I am an avid reader.

I have acquired many friends from all walks of life. I am often asked why I don't have a boyfriend. Well, why would I? I have my children and lots of good friends so I am content to be my own person I don't need a boyfriend and there's nothing I would do to change that?

I felt proud of myself to see how far I have come and how far I'm going to go. I'm like my mum a born survivor my family are my world.

It's been a few months now since my daughter Katie and I became reconciled and things are much better between us. She had previously been told she would never be able to conceive due to problems with her ovaries. However, on doing a pregnancy test recently she found out the test showed it was positive. It goes to prove the powers that be, don't always get it right. She carried to full term though without any problems.

She went in to labour and it lasted all night and all day. I stayed with her the whole time and I felt sure she would need to have a caesarean section. Although I'm terrible squeamish I went along and surprised myself as I watched the whole procedure. It was totally fascinating and finally little Harry was born weighing a grand nine and a half pounds. He looked like a little Chinese baby and had to be rushed into ICU because of his breathing. Katie was stitched up and taken back to the ward. She was very weak and ill after the birth and had to stay in hospital for three weeks until she felt strong enough to come home.

Once out of hospital little Harry and Katie spent two further weeks at home with me and it was so nice to be back together as a family. Harry brought so much love and joy to our lives and his Aunty Molly and Aunty Darcy make a great fuss of him and rightly so. We all think he has a look of Uncle Adam too so that made Adam feel included.

ADAM IS HOME ON LEAVE

It seemed such a long while but then he came home on leave for ten days. The time passed too quickly and the day before he was due back we attended the funeral of a good friend of Adam's. That night we got very drunk it was sad and I also didn't want to have to say goodbye to Adam again as he would be on his way back to Afghanistan.

Adam set off with his stuff in his backpack and we kissed and said goodbye. It was only a matter of time before he sent me a text to let me know he'd arrived in Afghanistan without one of his trainers. I went to the post office as soon as I could after finding it underneath his bed upstairs. When the postmaster asked what was in the parcel (which they have to ask). I said one mucky trainer! He laughed and laughed. Amazing how you make a friend of people and it did me good to have a laugh.

We were always in touch one way or another. Adam mailed us and sometimes sent us a video diary online for us and at the end of these videos he always said 'See you soon, Molly, Darcy and Mum'. Darcy loved him to say this.

The next time Adam came home for good after his tour ended. It was wonderful to see him home safe and sound and it being my birthday the best present ever. After having a six-month stint in Afghanistan they were allowed to have a holiday. Adam and some of his friends booked a holiday to Mexico and it was great for them to get away the lads deserved a holiday after all they'd seen and gone through.

Once Adam came back home from Mexico he gave me some money to buy a new stairs carpet which I needed as ours was almost threadbare. That is the way Adam has always been towards me, a kind and caring son.

It goes without saying once he returned we arranged a party for him and everyone got together at the pub we had one hell of a party everyone was happy and glad to have him back from Afghanistan and having survived the trauma of war.

His next post was to join his regiment back at the Wellington Barracks in London. He would be on duty at the Trooping of the Colour on the occasion of HRH Prince William and Catherine's wedding day. It doesn't get much better than this. I mean my son. The son I am so proud of was to be part of the big day of a royal wedding. I would have loved to be there to witness this but I know I wouldn't have been able to cope with being amongst such a great crowd. I would have felt claustrophobic and probably wouldn't have seen as much as I did by watching the spectacular event on television with my family from home.

Adam made so many great friends during his time in the army and they are still in touch with Adam and the family on Face book today.

Over that same period a holiday had been booked to Turkey, as usual it was with my good friend, Antony, he's just been such a great friend, and still is to this day. He absolutely loved all my kids so everything worked out just fine. There was never any romance between us; we have always been just great chums. My youngest daughter, Darcy, had gone away on holiday with her dad, which was good for both of them. It also gave me the opportunity to get away for a much needed break. This time we went to Antalya it was a very long coach tour but worth it. We all went on a boat trip it was amazing, however Antony had a bit of mishaps going down from the top deck and fell on top of a man, on the lower deck beneath us.

No-one had been hurt, thankfully, and to be honest everyone ended up having a great laugh. That was, after we'd realised that the guy he toppled on joined in as he saw the funny side to it all. It's always fun times with Anthony. We enjoyed the food and the country sightseeing. It was such a great and enjoyable holiday and did us all a great deal of good.

Three days into the holiday I received a message from my son, Adam, telling me he was going to Thailand for a holiday. I was a little shocked but I always wanted my kids to travel and enjoy life. Not to have to live the life I'd had. I asked him to keep in touch, we usually always do on messenger, even if it's a message or a picture sent.

For a further week I relaxed with my mate Antony spending time relaxing or going out exploring the Island. Along the way we met many people to chat to. Once we arrived home I was a little upset that Adam hadn't been in touch before he left for Thailand though it wasn't as if he was at the other side of the world.

The following week I returned to my cleaning job. I felt refreshed after my holiday and at last life was starting to feel great, I had secured a further cleaning job as well as that I began to make jewellery and oil burners at the Spiritual Church. I was happy to be amongst real people, the kind you can trust. I go along with my good friend Sarah each week.

Finally, I heard from Adam to say he was having a great time in Thailand. He told me he had met up with an old school friend who was travelling onwards to Australia so they decided to meet up in Bangkok.

Three days later there was a loud knock on my door. I looked through the curtains from downstairs, (something I always do). I saw a lady on the doorstep.

This was the day I was to get the biggest shock of my life.

MY WORLD IS TURNED UPSIDE DOWN

I opened the downstairs lounge window the lady seemed a little startled to see me at the widow, rather than opening the door To be honest this is a regular habit for me and something I tend to do when anyone calls, because of the many times I was on my own feeling vulnerable. Having had to deal with an abusive partner it made me feel safer to do this when a stranger is at the door and is not known to me.

I leaned out a little further not knowing why she was here. The stilted conversation went something along the lines of -

'Are you Karen Carter?' I replied, 'Yes'

'Do you have a son called Adam?'

Again I answered, 'Yes'.

'I need to speak to you,' she said.

I'd felt flustered and anxious as I made my way to the door. My youngest daughter Darcy was in the front room watching the television.

After opening the door and letting her into the front room I motioned her to take a seat and sit down. My head was spinning I didn't know what she was going to tell me.

'Is he dead?' I asked.

'No, he's in prison in Thailand.'

This happened on 16 September 2015 in Thailand. My nerves were all over the place, I couldn't stop crying and shaking. I went next door to my mum and dads sobbing my heart out. There was nothing I could do he was so far away.

I managed to go into work the Friday although I had hadn't slept much all night. I received a Face book call from someone in Thailand. I answered it and was shocked to hear Adams voice. He told me he was in the police station and looking at a twenty-three year sentence. I could only speak for a few seconds before the line went dead. One of my colleagues, Ann, took me home and tried to talk things through with me and gave me some sound advice.

When my phone pinged I picked it up, there was a message from the British Embassy. The message I read said. '*Your son is in prison, please ring this number.*'

I did as the message had instructed me to do and then I waited and waited for a call back. It was torture for me as I paced up and down the house I was beside myself with worry about my son. Then I started to receive clips online of pictures coming out of Bangkok. The story was all over the Thailand papers. The pictures clearly depicted on CCTV my son and his friend exchanging £100 notes.

I have changed the name of Adam's friend to Ben and another lad called Tom. They had met up in Bangkok. It appears that Ben had been in Thailand a few weeks and to be honest he was known to people back in Burnley his home town as not having a good reputation. I'm not one to judge anyone because nobody is perfect. I'm only telling you this to perhaps explain the situation a little more.

We had a family get together with my parents and the parents of the other boys' family. It was decided that the boys' fathers would go over to Thailand and enquire about getting legal representation for the lads. Days after this meeting a friend of mine turned up and gave me £500 for my fare over to Thailand. My friend Sarah booked my flight for me and within the hour I packed a small bag and we on my way to the airport. I was literally terrified. I had never travelled this far in my entire life.

First I had to travel from Manchester then had a stay over in London before travelling on to Thailand. I was scared on my own and working on autopilot. I then got a call from Ben's mum screaming abuse down the phone at me. '*You, get the fuck back home*,' she shouted.

I switched my mobile phone off then tried to get some sleep. Heading off to the airport early morning I sat there watching the cleaner polishing windows for seven hours with my phone off. I had plenty of time to think and I was feeling I would have to accept the fact that my son could be spending twenty-three years in prison.

Because of the emotional state I was in I felt constantly sick. I sat there for a long while watching the normal life of others going about the airport.

They were happy people living their dreams, all jetting off to many holiday destinations, looking happy and excited.

The flight I was on would take nine hours. Every hour that passed I cried then stop and then cried again. I couldn't stop myself I think with all that had happened in the space of a few days it was obvious I was suffering from shock. For a while I did enjoy the peace and quiet as I sat there in my own space.

Whilst waiting to board the aircraft to Bangkok all I saw was happy faces travelling on the same flight as me and looking forward to a holiday in Thailand. After eating a substantial amount of food (I hadn't eaten much in days) I pulled a blanket over my head, kept myself to myself and spoke to no-one.

Arriving at Bangkok airport I was even more scared the airport is enormous. Somehow I managed to find the correct terminal, which would take me to Koi Samui. When the plane landed at its destination thankfully it was a very tiny airport so I had felt a little relieved that I would be able to find my way around and not, hopefully, get lost.

I went over to the taxi rank and asked to be taken to the address the boys' parents were staying in out there. On arrival at the hotel I asked the women about the two men I was looking for. She didn't appear to know who I was looking for and began to show me pictures of two Russian men. I was petrified that I'd landed at the wrong place and the wrong hotel. Thankfully, a girl approached me and directed me over to where there are some rented bungalows and told me that perhaps that's where I needed to be.

I was totally relieved as I walked up to the shed (reception) place close to the bungalows and when I asked the gentleman if he knew the two men in question namely Tony and Ian. He looked up and asked.

'Are you Karen?'

The sweat poured out of me, finally, at last, it had dawned on me, that I had found the right place, and not only that, the lovely guy in front of me had put me at my ease with his big smile and had given me the kindest welcome, it was such a relief. So much so, I'd dashed over to him and given him a great big hug, liked he'd been a long-lost family member. He informed me the other dads who'd arrived earlier than me, had gone to visit the boys in prison and they had left a message for me to say they would be seeing Adam and passing on the good news that I had arrived, and that hopefully, I would be over to the prison as soon as it could be arranged.

Then the rain arrived, it belted down, I don't think I've ever seen rain like that in my life before. The man in the shed was very hospitable offering me a drink until the men returned. On their return they informed me that they were all being looked after well and not being mistreated at all and that made me feel better. I met Tania and her brother who arranged a room for me to stay whilst I was there. I made plans to visit Adam at the Koh Somui District Prison the following day.

Once at the prison we found out that the Embassy had put the wrong names on the board so we had to return and email them to get it sorted out for us and then we were able to return I was so frustrated by not being able to go in and see my son after all the hours of travelling.

Sitting there in the waiting room where we had to show our passports I looked down the pathway to the prison and could see Buffaloes in a field and a monkey wild and free. I felt drained with the heat and emotional and to be honest a still felt nervous and a bit scared.

Then the big metal door slid open and there they were behind the glass. My heart almost stopped it was such a momentous feeling to see him at last. He reassured me they were looking after him all right and I kept on telling him I would do anything I could to help him. The meeting wasn't long and seemed to pass so quickly but I reassured him I would be back the following day. We bought fresh fruit and water for them before leaving and returning back to the place we were all staying.

Once I'd returned to my room I sobbed myself to sleep. The following day I was still in shock, in *no man's land,* so, I took a walk outside. I was enthralled by the wonderful scenery and the beach, it was so restful and with the sun on my face I could hardly take in what a beautiful country I was in. For a while I'd simply allowed myself to soak it all up, it felt so tranquil and had calmed me down a little.

The food was excellent and I tucked into it and for the first time in a long while I ate well. I did obviously think about and miss my daughters. I took comfort in the music my taste was of Aretha Franklin and Amy Winehouse and then Red Hot Chilli Peppers. I sat for hours at the edge of the beach amazed by the view. I felt rather calm yet at the same time numb. I sent messages home to my friends and daughters.

As I sat on the doorstep trying to connect to the internet, I found out that a male friend of mine had died and another had a bad accident. I thought to myself, at least my son is alive and this gave me hope.

We travelled back to the prison to meet a lawyer who told us he would represent the three boys. We had to sign papers and when we asked about bail and was told there was only a 20 per cent chance they would get it. The cost for each of the three lads would be £7,000 each. If at the end of it, if bail is refused, they do not return this money. After speaking to our lads they told us not to go ahead with bail.

It was put on social media that we had given up but this was all untrue. Who on earth gives up on the child even when they are adults? It was heartbreaking and my tears at this stage had run dry. The worst part of all was when it came to say goodbye to Adam from behind a glass window. It was awful not to be able to give him a hug and try to reassure him.

My flight back home was from a different airport than the other two men. First I flew to Singapore and had a long seven hour wait to get my flight back to Manchester. I'd sat there holding on to the very few clothes of Adams I was taking back with me. Most of his belongings like his watch had been stolen off him. I felt sad as I waited for my flight and couldn't stop crying, yet again, I seem to always be in a time warp of tears.

Finally, I made my way on to the flight back to Manchester; I felt I wanted to be left alone. Then a child who was seated next to me began crying loudly. I asked one of the crew if it was possible to move. She managed to get me seated at the back with curtain around me. I stayed there I was in a dreadful emotional state until the plane landed.

After I had come through Customs I made my way to the arrivals hall. Standing there waiting for me was my friend Sarah and Janet a woman from the spiritual church and I never been more happy to see anyone in my life. We hugged each other over and over; I must have looked a right sight having cried all the way back but it was good to be home. I couldn't wait now to see Molly and Darcy, mum and dad and my dog. I still felt bad about not having done much to help Adam or for that matter if I would see him again.

RETURNING TO THAILAND

After getting home we arranged a meeting to discuss what questions we needed to ask our lawyer (who only seemed interested in money!) We got no information regarding our questions and decided to sack her. We had little or no help from the Home Office. It felt like the end of the world for me.

Then out of the blue Ben got bail. Unbelievable! He got in touch with me and said I should go back with ten thousand pounds and he would meet me there and would get Adam out of prison.

I believed with Ben having got home it would make it worse for the other two left behind and they may both get an even longer sentence.

I'm a very trusting person and so I was ready to do whatever I could so it came as I great shock to wake up the following morning to see Ben on social media. He was stood outside Heathrow airport back in English soil! I wrote a message online, telling him to *rot in hell.* I was absolutely fuming. Who wouldn't be? My emotions were all over the place; truly I do not know how I held it together at all.

I had no intention of parting company with Ian and Tony the other parents, after all we are a team and very supportive of each other.

I was unable to work I lacked energy. I had nothing to hang on to, no hope at all. I cried even more buckets of tears when listening to songs on the radio whilst drinking coffee after coffee to keep me going. I had given up smoking but now I was smoking like a chimney and not eating. My family were really concerned about my health.

We had a family chat group on WhatsApp that helped to keep me sane. There were family members who went over to see the boys and one relative lives out there so he went to see Adam.

I wrote so many letters trying to do something. Then the King of Thailand died and my letters ceased to be delivered. I only received one email a week of 15 lines long off Adam. This was the only contact I had with him.

I was constantly sick and then I found out the army who was supposed to be paying Adam a wage until Christmas had stopped all payments. As you can imagine his account was overdrawn just to add to the troubles.

It seems incredible that the army did nothing whatsoever to help Adam. He'd spent seven years of his life serving his country a big part of that in risking his life in Afghanistan. I never so much got a phone call from the army and when I tried to speak to someone they passed me a telephone number which turned out to be the number of the camp dentist!

It had taken a lot of time and effort to get the amount of bail money together. This would not have happened if people hadn't come forward to help us. My dad provided some of the money and the Spiritual Church held a night with a medium present and the church collected over £800. Many times I would open my front door to complete strangers who pressed money in my hand to help with getting Adam home. I was so choked up and emotional to realise how many kind people there are here in Burnley. Friends of Adam's set up a fund online which raised an amount of £700. All of the money we collected was split between us. The flights cost £700 each and the bail money ran into thousands.

Finally, I set off to Thailand only this time I was accompanied. We'd intended to get there and do our best to get bail for Adam. Only my parents and a few close friends knew where I was going. Everyone else thought I was going to Scotland. It was all cloak and dagger stuff. I felt absolutely terrible having to lie to everyone but at the time I couldn't trust anyone the fact I was returning to Thailand.

On arrival we met a man who I will refer to as Pete he was married to a Thai lady. To be honest I was scared because we were carrying a very large amount of money. It was raining and as we travelled through many dark streets. I was feeling nervous. I only had a Barclays Bank pen on me I expect that wasn't much of a weapon if we were to be attacked.

After trying to get into conversation and trying to suss him out. He finally stopped and said we would be staying at the accommodation where he'd parked the car. It didn't look a very nice area so we insisted we wanted to stay in Koi Samui where I'd stayed at my previous visit. Eventually we were dropped off there.

Going to the shed (reception) there was no-one around and so we had to resign ourselves to the fact we would be spending the night sleeping in reception on the chairs and settee. In the morning a man appeared in reception, he was the owner and thought we were leaving. How kind it was of him, not only to find us a room, but a lovely room at a much cheaper rate I had previously paid.

Later that morning Pete arrived and took us to court to apply for bail. Then I waited and waited and paced and paced the floor drinking can after can of Chang to keep cool. Then there was a knock-knock and the door opened and standing there right in front of me was Adam. What a turnabout. I ran to him and hugged and hugged him. After all that time inside and to be honest with the heat he didn't smell too sweet but he was out! That's all I ever wanted, to have him out of that prison. That night we painted the town red and who could blame us enjoying a curry and a few drinks it was just wonderful.

The following day Pete goes into court to get the passports sorted. We got ripped off by having to pay for them. We should have got them back for free!

Nothing mattered to us though now we had the lads back. It was decided that Ian would travel to Cambodia for seventeen hours in a taxi. Ian was a member of the family who lives on another island in Thailand and helped us as much as he could. Tony and I decided we would stay somewhere else for the night. It was then we received the phone call we had been dreading from Cambodia. It appears Ian passed through customs without a problem then Adam handed over his passport and boom! It flashes up he is not to leave the island. They grabbed their passports and ran out and took another taxi back to Bangkok.

It had been arranged we would all meet up in Pattaya. We had to take a boat trip which took an hour and a half and then a flight back to Bangkok and finally a two-hour taxi drive before we all met up. The hotel we stayed in that night was possibly the worse hotel I've ever stayed in, it was filthy dirty and disgusting and painted bright purple, I think Trip Adviser would have had a field day! Obviously, we were not on a holiday or in the country to enjoy ourselves.

The next person we met up with who I will refer to as Lenny was our next link to getting the boys home. Pattaya was a place I can only describe as a type of Blackpool, but worse. (Sorry Blackpool, no offence). Off we went to meet up with Lenny in a strip club. I was the only girl there wearing clothes, strange and amusing in a way but it wasn't important, what was important was to sort out getting the boys out of the country, it would be very risky.

Off they went again on another seventeen-hour taxi ride. It would have been too expensive for us all to go so Tony and I stayed behind. We spent time walking around; I was looking for a lead for my phone. I hated lying to my family about being in Scotland and everything was getting to me. Because of our anxieties we ended up bitching at one another about nothing. I was anxious all the time and worried and found myself having to take Valium which I got over the counter from the chemist and music still was helping me to cope.

We had to make out way back so off we went to the airport. We flew to Dohi it was such a massive place I'd never seen anything like it. Then, it had been another flight back home to Manchester. I remember the empty seat between Tony and I, the seat should have been occupied by Ian. We decided to put a cushion on the seat and strapped it in. The woman seated behind us kept giving us funny looks. I don't think anyone would believe the journey we had been on together.

Once we landed at Manchester I received a text message from the boys to say they had got through Malaysia.

With a heavy heart I made my way home to mum and dads. It was the 5th of November and Darcy was at a bonfire with my friend Sarah. Molly had gone out. I remember dad bought me a pizza and then I returned to my own home where I fell fast asleep but awoke instantly the minute I heard my phone ping. The boys were on English soil at last. They had landed in London and were on their way back home by bus.

Months and months of worrying and at last we were all together the relief was beyond words.

THE JUSTICE SYSTEM

The Thai Justice System is brutal but also big business and in many cases they can as brutal as they possibly can. The police, lawyers, guards and prison directors will cheat you out of your money. In fact you don't have to commit a crime to find yourself in prison. Often it's a case of being in the wrong place at the wrong time.

Generally speaking if a dispute arises between a person from Thailand and a foreigner the foreigner is automatically arrested. It is not a case of not liking the foreigner it all about the opportunity to get as much money from them as they can. The chances are the foreigner will be put inside a jail often with the threat of long prison sentences. Of course, with this over their heads, relatives will do anything to get them out of jail and one way or another get hold of the cash to get them released.

Thailand is an amazing place to spend a holiday in yet also it can become a nightmare if you fall on the wrong side of their laws. Your life can be put on the line and the death penalty is something you may have to face.

Compared to England the laws here are far more relaxed when compared to Thailand but each country has their own way to run their land.

The punishment for drugs can be extremely severe like being imprisoned for life or even worse the death sentence.

A former British citizen was sentenced to fifty years for drug dealing in Thailand. He was carrying 200 ecstasy tablets which were found on him in Pattaya. Hoping for a lighter sentence he pleaded guilty but the final sentence was fifty years in a prison called Klong Prem – Central Prison Bangkok without parole. His parents appealed for a lighter sentence fearing for his safety in the squalid horrendous prison.

Living with cockroaches under their feet whilst being fed rotten rice and fish heads. Prisoners sleep on the concrete floor along with approximately 74 other prisoners in a cell block designed for 20.

An Englishman was arrested in November 2011 at a bar in Pattaya. A Thai lawyer advice was for him to plead guilty. The outcome was that he was jailed for three years. He was charged with selling Viagra and Steroids online. The business had been up and running for six years. He was put into the Nong Pala Jail and locked up inside with him. One of them was jailed for stealing whisky from a Supermarket. Within a week one of them was beaten to death. All food and blankets had to be paid for. His meagre rations were tinned sardines or chicken foot and cold rice.

This man also states that the corruption over there is unbelievable and that the English Embassy over there was of little assistance to him. When he questioned this with them they told him they were aware of his arrest and provided assistance.

Again in England the rules here are much more relaxed.

The prison where my son was imprisoned was holding 600/800 inmates at Samui District Prison. The prisoners have a shortage of water in jail. (No rights or wrongs here? This is the jail where it's a case of (*no money no honey as they say)*

It is vital for the prisoners to buy fruit to provide themselves with important vitamins. If the prisoners are not able to buy fruit then over a number of months they begin to suffer with scurvy a very unpleasant skin disease.

As from July 2015 prison visitors are not allowed to take in food or books into prison. They are, however, allowed, (provided they show their ID), to purchase food and deposit money for them.

The prison population is increasing all the time there are on average 40 inmates to a 24 square metre cell, previously 30sq m a year ago. Prisoners are supported and anyone can donate to buy water with Pay Pal email: kohsamurinmatess@gmail.com .

In our experience on arrival to visit our sons we were frustrated and confused as the paperwork was not in place for us to see them. We had to return to the hotel and get in touch with the Embassy returning later that day for our visit.

Conditions are dire in the end it all about mental strength and finding you place in the system. Newcomers go through waves of being freaked out by their surroundings. The long timers have a calmness that seems to say: 'I've seen it all and I accept my fate'. Back in England every prisoner deserves to have basic food and water and somehow seem to think they are badly done to. This is not what our boys would have ever believed could have happened to be placed in such degradation in this prison situation.

We now feel lucky to have got our boys back home and away from the mistreatment.

I have been asked many times if I would return to Thailand and the answer is yes, I would love to return someday if only to sample their street food and to visit wonderful sights such as The Temple. Also the amazing beaches I did get a glimpse at and of course all the animals which roam about this land, wonderful.

People seem surprised to hear I would return after my experience of getting my son home which wasn't want I would have wanted but their law is their law and we just have to move on now. There were so many lovely people who were kind to me and as I mentioned it is such a beautiful country apart from the strict laws. People back in England don't get the death penalty even if they kill someone at variance with Thailand but that's the way it is maybe England are too soft but maybe Thailand are harsh.

Since getting back home and speaking with Adam he told me what the routine was whilst he was incarcerated.

At six pm he woke up to a bell, then the cells are unlocked and then they count everyone. There are 45 people all waiting to use the toilet and there is only one toilet for all of them.

At eight pm they have to sing the National Anthem followed by Buddhist prayers then a second counting of prisoners.

Everyone goes downstairs where to hear the National Anthem played on recorders into microphones and everyone stands in lines before being counted again.

After the 8am count on weekdays only you put on prison uniform until l.00pm blue uniform for convicts and brown for people on remand. The count of prisoners happens at 11.00 am l.00pm and 4.00pm during the week.

The prison shop opens after the 8.00pm count but they do not serve until 9.00am. Goods are fairly basic like soap, razors etc. also biscuits and soft drinks.

Every twelve days they make you shave then shackles are put in place then a hoop of metal over your foot which is extremely uncomfortable.

At 8.30am you are served a breakfast of nasty looking rice foul smelling broth with bones in. This is also served at dinner and if you're lucky you get some small pieces of chicken in the broth.

Most of the farangs and other inmates order food from the outside. These are made the day before. A business man named Amon who is half Thai, half Italian and lived in Germany. He takes a surcharge for every ordered taken. It can take as ten minutes up to a long two hours queuing for this service.

At 11.00am they stand for the count, once they have been counted they have to crouch down, many young juveniles inmates tend to flick elastic bands or toss stones, which gives a kind of idea of their IQ.

This would be the normal type of day for Adam whilst he was there:-.

At 11.45am Lunch – Ordered out food was brought in usually breaded chicken or a dish call Khao Mok Gai – yellow chicken yellow rice or sandwiches.

1.00pm - A count takes place then the inmates can spend time chatting, resting or exercising in a makeshift gym. Basically concrete blocks on metal bar – imagine a Fred Flintstones gym.

At 2.00/3.00pm Showers open there are only two troughs so if you happen to be late then there is no water left.

Dinner at 3.00pm followed free time which is boring –
occasionally they can see the mountain from the yard.
At 4.00pm we go back to the cell.

Smoking is allowed downstairs but cigarette lighters are
not allowed. Adam and the inmates were only allowed
water and a book. Lock up was from 4.30pm until
5.30pm.

Finally at 9.30pm locked up in your cell. The lights are
left on all night and you are not allowed to make any
noise

There is no comparison with prisons in England; you
think prisons in England are bad?

These are some of the Thailand rules that are punishable by
jail:-

1.   Do not defile any image of the Thai King – this
      includes defacing Thai money. You must not step
      on any baht (Thai currency). This is   against
      Thai law resulting in 3 to 15 years in prison.

   2 Thai law requires that tourists have their ID on them
   at all times.

   3 Never leave your passport with anyone when renting
a motorbike.

   4   In Thailand it is illegal to leave the house with no
   underwear on.

   5   You will be fined up to £400 if you throw chewing
   gum in the street

Penalty for not paying the fine is jail.

In Thailand driving a car with no shirt on is illegal also.

There are a few people along the way I felt and still feel resentment towards, not the least the British Army who did nothing to help an ex-soldier in his hour of need. They cut off his wages when money was desperately needed to get him out of prison also whenever we tried to speak to anyone they were never available. Even since Adam returned home they are not prepared to forward an exemplary reference after serving eight loyal years fighting for his country. They have turned a proud mum into an angry mum but I'm trying to move on.

The people who helped so much outweigh the nasty people. Without the good people in the world I don't know what we would have done. Getting Adam home was the objective and I can only thank all of the many people who helped from the bottom of my heart. So many people Amber, Jess the list goes on and on.

LIFE GOES ON

My daughter, Molly, had trained to become a hairdresser and then she decided to become a butcher, she had tried so many jobs. However, she totally enjoyed the butchery job; having worked there from the age of fourteen as a Saturday girl, she loved it. So at this juncture she was happy enough working in the Market Hall at Andrew's Butchery stall. For now, at least, she had settled to a job she liked and enjoyed having plenty of banter with all the customers she was happy to serve the public.

I am still keeping up my keep fitness regime I took up hula hooping. I ended up swinging three rings around and became quite good at it but found it a great form of keeping fit, I enjoyed it. My life was becoming happier and more settled, living a normal simple life.

In the main, things had been going well and I had decided to help at the food bank with packing and deliveries around the town of Burnley, for families who at that time were experiencing money difficulties. I'd met some real characters along the way. I go out on deliveries with a lovely person called Elaine who was also a street pastor. I have so much respect for Elaine, who goes into town at nights to help the people living rough and people who are without friends or some of them are alcoholics. I am still in touch with Elaine today what a dedicated and good person she is.

I had still been attending the spiritualist church meetings twice a week and was able to afford to go away on holiday once a year.

ADAM SETTLES INTO CIVILIAN LIFE

Having returned from Thailand we had to think of the best way to pay off the debts. Adam opened an online fund raising app and this raised £500 which truly helped a lot. Then the Spiritual Church set up an evening of mediums and shared the profits with us.

Things began to settle down for him and I'm hoping the drama is at an end. I certainly feel as though I've aged fifty years. Looking back I can only say the people of Thailand who helped us so much were the friendliest and most caring people I've ever met and I would love to go back one day as it is a beautiful country. I do have some treasured memories of Thailand though the reason for being there had been agonising at times we got through and I can now look back with love in my heart for the people.

Without music in my life I'm sure it helped me as much as anything. Red Hot Chilli's, Stone Roses and oh so many more kept me sane! I'm still recovering and to be honest my life has been a real trial at times. I have now have my faith and love in my life and I will survive, I fear no-one I work hard and I want to express how the Spiritual Church gave me so much support throughout.

My dream came true when my son, Adam managed to get hold of tickets for four of us to go to a concert to see… YES! At last it's time for The Stone Roses on stage.'

I could hardly sleep the night before I was like a kid waiting for Father Christmas feeling excited and happy. It turned out to be one of the best experiences of my life. We caught the bus to Manchester and then made our way to Heaton Park where the concert was to be held. The atmosphere was manic everyone feeling the love of the Stone Roses. Fans joined in together along the way jostling and mixing like long lost friends.

This was an experience I can feel any time I want to just by thinking of the brilliant day and I felt so blessed to be there.

On arriving at the park we had to be searched by men wearing official jackets. Scott, a friend of Adam and who was part of our party had concealed two bottles of Buckfast Scottish wine and hidden them in his Wellington boots. I couldn't stop laughing as we all watched him making his way to be searched. His legs looked as bandy as bent boomerang as he strode out looking like Jack Wayne without his horse!

Oh! Jesus, I laughed so much I wet myself. Even security laughed as it was obvious to them where Scott had hidden the bottles. His cover was blown and there was no getting through the gate with any drink today.

Security gave him the option of taking the wine off him or he could drink it. We were laughing once more as we looked at Scott wondering what he would do.

'No Way!' Scott laughed.

He pulled both bottles in quick succession from his Wellies, then downed both bottles one after the other! Finally, we made our way across the field only this time Scott's demeanour had changed. Instead of looking like he'd just dismounted a horse he was now wobbling in his Wellies! I think we laughed all day long.

Arriving in a good spot nearest to the stage where the *Stone Roses* would be appearing we lucky enough to find the perfect place which gives us a bird's eye view of everything.

'Brilliant, Bring It on!'

Thirty minutes later we looked behind us and the crowds were there in their thousands all out to make the most of the concert.

First to come on stage was Liam Gallagher who sang a few of Oasis favourites and then at last the Stone Roses singing Fools Gold. Absolutely amazing rendition the crowds went wild. There's the biggest grin on my face even thinking about it. Truly great!

A year later I went again with a friends' husband to see them but somehow they had lost some of the magic for me and didn't reach the heights I was looking forward too, maybe it was me who had changed, I really do not know but I know without a doubt the Stone Roses got me through many tragic situations over a long period of time. Long may they live!

There's also many people at home who have done so much for me I can never thank them enough, my boss who allowed me time off work to go to Thailand, my family, the Spiritual Church, the list is never ending. Thank you to all.

It's going to be Christmas soon and I feel I can move forward with the love of my family and friends around me the world is a wonderful place at the moment!

All I ever wanted in my life is peace of mind. I enjoy a lot of things like reading and going for long walks in the hills near where I live. I do this at least two times a week even in winter.

I've worn our three pairs of trainers. It keeps me focussed and more alert.

Since arriving back home to Burnley, Adam got a job working for a friends' dad. I couldn't stop laughing when he told me his work required him to watch the machine churning out plastic tubs. He said he only looked away for a minute or two and when he turned back the tubs were piling up all over the place top of each other. Having had a similar experience with cardboard boxes I knew exactly what he meant. He was obviously not used to working in a factory situation. Needless to say the job didn't last.

Adam has since acquired another job in engineering which is well paid and he appears to have settled at last.

Tom, his friend who experienced the prison life also is now in full time work and appears to be doing well.

Luke, the other friend who travelled with them has moved away from Burnley. I saw him prior to his leaving town and we hugged each other. We had gone through such harrowing experiences and thankfully they are back home at least and able to carry on normal life.

Sadly all the lads just happened to be in the wrong place at the wrong time and paid the price for that. I doubt any of them will forget being imprisoned at

Koi Samui District Prison and the disgusting interior of that place and treatment they had and terrible food not to mention the sights they saw in there.

For me also it was an experience I never want to experience again. You never know what trials you face in life but I did gain experience in travelling a long distance on my own and had found the confidence to travel to London on my own to see Adam. In some ways it was the worst thing you can imagine to happen to anyone yet I did feel a special spiritual connection to Thailand and its people. The country is a beautiful though it does have a hidden agenda.

TIME TO MOVE ON

Things have return to some sort of normality since returning from Thailand I have been busy trying to get my cleaning business off the ground. It's not been easy as I had to take so much time off with getting Adam out of prison in Thailand. I did lose one of my customers. Although the others were extremely kind to me and now I am able to pick up where I left off.

Just as my life was jogging along in a more normal and happy phase something always seems to cut through all that - like The Council Tax.

The Benefit System

To start with I began to receive not one but four council tax forms with all differing figures. I'm not against paying my bills but this was confusing for me. My income was exactly the same as the year before and although I have a government business adviser I can contact I find it all too stressful when I try to get help when I make a call to the council offices. Why? I ask myself, what can I do about it? Being self-employed I find myself worse of then if I was on benefits and I must say the adviser was of no help at all when I ask for an explanation. I feel they could do with lessons in how to conduct business on a telephone and learn how to be polite to their customers for a start.

In between my cleaning job, writing my book, doing voluntary work and being a mum, I also have regular visits to see the Council Tax Office in fact I've visited so often now we are on first name terms!

Life is so funny at times I have been working on a voluntary basis at the local Hospice shop for a few months and the people we get in there are extremely interesting to listen and talk too. Amusingly I've had many proposals of marriage or dates that's coming from the over 70s mostly older than my own dad!

The takings have doubled since my friend Carrie and I became a team and am now working together. I've known Carrie for over twenty years and we have such fun working together in the Hospice shop. It's hilarious at times, so many colourful people come in and we have such a good banter with them. I'm sure many of them come in to be cheered up and have a laugh.

The sales figures are good and we both love the interaction with the customers who are in the main, young at heart and always have stories to tell. Quite often our shop manager Sally looks at the two of us and shakes her head, I think she may think we are slightly mental but on the whole we get along famously. Only a week ago one of the many regular shoppers left me some chocolates and a lovely card. I was really choked up by the kindness of people. It's so worthwhile and I can honestly say I look forward to going there.

You wouldn't believe it but some of the seniors actually ask if there's any discount, you have to laugh but they always copper up and buy something and go away smiling. Carrie is a Jane MacDonald fan and even looks like her and dresses like her. My nickname for her though is David Dickinson when she picks up an eye glass to examine clothing to see if it's active and crawling. I laugh so much at her it's such a tonic and the customers join in with us. The old folks always say to us that laughter is the best medicine and I couldn't agree more.

It was during the time when Adam was locked up in Thailand jail that Carrie asked me to be a bridesmaid at her wedding. I'd never been a bridesmaid so it was lovely for her to ask me and I couldn't refuse but there was a cloud over me all day worrying about what was happening to Adam. I managed to struggle though the day in my high heeled shoes and then hobbled my away home and the minute I got through my front door my shoes were off and I flopped in the chair exhausted.

With everything which has happened to me during the past twelve months not to mention what my life has been like over the past 40 years or so I began to think seriously about writing it all down.

I knew without a doubt this was going to be one of the hardest tasks of my life, although I loved reading and still do, unfortunately due to missing so much schooling I felt the prospect of writing a biography would be daunting.

Yet I've always tried to be a positive thinker and usually get on with things and once I set my mind to it I decided I would try and find a way. I wanted desperately to get it all out of my mind and transferred into print. First of all I went to the library and found a local writing group here in Burnley called the Burnley & District Writers' Circle.

At the first meeting I found a guardian angel called Joyce, she had volunteered to help me if she could, by typing my scripts or give an account of my past, warts and all. I'd hoped to end up with a best seller, but that was me, always the dreamer. Joining this group had certainly built up a sense of confidence in me. I was always apologising for my writing and wondering if I would be judged.

However, they are not a group who sit there in judgement on anyone; we all have a book inside us so we are told. They welcomed me, and I had found them to be a lovely group of people and also I had been given so much help by listening to criticism of mine work and their pieces of work. It appeared, everyone joins a group with trepidation, yet I was never made to an outcast. They gave me help with critiques and suggestions of how to improve on my writing, but never judgemental. It was a group for people with a genuine interest in writing. Burnley Writers' are still going strong today, though I did have to leave as I had a young family still at home and it was difficult for me on a Saturday.

I loved to hear the stories they write and what critiques they get from the rest of the members. Many of them were excellent writers and their work is creative and interesting. At times, the class, on occasion have a great sense of humour so there was always times when one of them had written something extremely amusing and every one would laugh hysterically, it broke up the seriousness of writing and I had always enjoyed my short membership with them. My piece at the last meeting we had to writing an amusing story. I had been inspired to write a short piece about a lady who often visited the Charity Shop where I'd worked on a voluntary basis. The lady in questioned was absolutely besotted by Elvis Presley so much, she'd had named her dog named Elvis. After reading it out the group appeared to have enjoyed my story and had laughed along with me in a good way.

RULES AND REGULATIONS

Cleaning jobs would not have been my first choice of a career. Clearing out fire places, filling coal buckets up with wood, polishing dusting, hovering, whatever work I had done made me feel proud that I was doing and job and not claiming benefits, which if I had done would have worked out I would have received more money than actually me going out to do my self-employed work to be honest.

It was not the life I wanted to live, staying at home and living of the country, and whilst I could have settled for this, I felt better to be going out and earning my own money. The truth when it came down to it meant that taking that choice, I had ended up with a suitcase full of council tax bills, all of which stated I owed them conflicting amounts of money. None, of them appeared to be for the same amount. It was totally, absurd.

It's not as if I have ever lived a lavish lifestyle, I had been scraping a living just to keep the wolf from the door. After having contacted the council, on more than one occasion, and getting extremely frustrated, I would end up crying in frustration by trying to get them to understand what my predicament was at that time. Finally, after not getting anywhere with them by phone, I had decided to sit down quietly and write a letter to the Head Officer of Burnley Council. It may not do me any good but I certainly felt better for writing it all down.

My heart goes out to the people who have to face going to the Job Centre. The rules are so strict that even if they go along to ask for help and assistance they find themselves speaking to insensitive staff most of the time, who appear to get pleasure out of inflicting more hardship on the jobless by threatening them with sanctions.

Having helped out as a voluntary worker at the food bank in Burnley I have listened to and seen what happens to the poorest members of society. If their benefits are sanctioned and stopped, for one reason or another it's mostly due to not signing on every week. Or more commonly, not having access to a computer.. Although the food banks do help the needy the supplies would barely feed the family for the week.

One of the main reasons why people are sanctioned is due to not having access to a computer. Those claiming dole money are expected to somehow have access to the internet. Many, as you might well understand do not own a computer and therefore they are told to go to the library, where you pay by the hour. They may have to wait up to an hour before one of the computers become free. Then each and every one of them only get one hour to do there searches.

The rule indicates that on a weekly basis a person has to prove they've applied for job vacancies and need to make a list to prove this. If they do not comply with the rules, they are immediately sanctioned, and receive no money at all and will need to apply again once they do comply with the rules. This can take up to six weeks to achieve. Six weeks is a very long time to wait when you have a family to feed, and that's when many have to resort to the food banks or they would starve.

I have witness with my own eyes on one occasion, when I was there, at the Job Centre. I saw a man who was so frustrated with the staff and the system for not understanding his situation. They barely lift their heads when he tries to speak to them, he feels intimidated by their attitude. They don't appear to even be listening to him as he tried to explain what his problem had been. The staff member he was trying to communicate with, talked over him and kept on telling him the rules. Told there would be no extenuating circumstances and then being dismissed must have driven him to the edge. There was absolutely no compassion shown towards him, which to me seemed totally wrong. In desperation the man exploded, picked something up threw it at the window. The window broke and the police were called and he was led away.

The majority of people watching all this could not have believed the treatment which was handed out to him. I personally felt like crying for the desperate situation he was in with no understanding at all from those behind the counters.

Another time I was at the Job Centre when a young girl sat down next to me. She was wearing her pyjamas. I whispered to her.

'Are you okay, why are you wearing your nightwear?'

She was doubled up in pain and had her arms wrapped around her stomach. As she struggled to breathe, she said. 'I've come here by taxi.'

'Why on earth didn't you ring up and explain to them?' That would have been what most people would have done, surely?' I thought.

I had been absolutely flabbergasted when she'd explained her circumstances to me.

'I did ring up but they said my money would be stopped if I didn't come to the Job Centre to sign on.'

What a terrible experience for a young girl to have to endure, which only confirms my belief after witnessing two separate incidents at the Job Centre these people must be made of stone, how heartless is that?

Then the girl leaned over and told me.

'I've come here by taxi from my hospital bed, I have to undergo an operation this afternoon and I'm terrified.'

I felt choked up and emotional for her but did my best to show her some compassion. I also offered her my place in the queue.

I did understand, of course, that there are some people out there who do not wish to work and try it on. But to see people coming into the job centre who are disabled many wheelchair bound people with missing limbs and many people with walking sticks who, clearly are not fit enough to work, who get the same drilling from the staff. Being told they have been assessed by a medical examination put in place by the Benefit Office (not even medically trained doctors) that many of these disabled people are deemed to be fit for work and do not qualify to be in the benefits system.

Ridiculous question asked of a man with a broken arm!

'Can you pick up a pen?'

I have a friend who has worked all his life and has been struck down with diabetes and has to have regular dialysis as his kidneys are failing. He also has had to have a leg amputated. He has to go on regular medicals to check his fitness for work. Surely this man has enough to deal with three days on dialysis not to mention the threat of dying if his kidney problem deteriorates. This is an extreme case of a man having to undergo such medicals, hasn't he suffered enough?

It truly upsets me to watch this type of treatment being dished out to not only the disabled but the young people as well, some of them undergoing cancer treatments. Words fail me. Do these people live in the real world?

I believe money should be spent on projects like employing some unemployed people to teach mothers or young girls or men, for that matter, how to cook meals on a budget. The unemployment benefit does not stretch that far but although I'm

Still not earning a fortune I've been able to make my money stretch further due to making economically healthy foods like vegetable soups with fresh vegetable, home-made chicken soup – making pans of corned beef hash, which can keep a family going with a meal for a few days. So, meals can be made more cheaply if you're prepared to spend time chopping vegetables and opening a tin of corned beef. Not everyone is capable or may never have been given support, or help in learning how to cook cheaply. In my case I had to learn quickly, it had been a must, or we would've gone hungry!

Having witnessed what people have to do to survive was an eye opener for me. Over the four years I worked there I met people from all walks of life even the better off people who, through no fault of their own, had hit a bad patch in their lives and if it hadn't have been for the supply of food from the Food Bank they and their families would have starved. Even so I saw for myself how the majority of people still managed to keep their chins up and try to hold on to their pride in this unfortunate time in their lives.

Whilst I worked there, we often received tins without labels so it was good to try to work out what would be inside. Once I took home a tin which I was sure contained beans. On opening it though it turned out to be peaches. Still, I like fruit and it's one of your five a day. Very important to eat fruit and vegetables, I always try to keep my family eating foods which are good for them. I do miss the mystery tins though I always enjoyed surprise when each tin was opened.

Poverty can hit at any time. It can happen to rich or poor. People's lives can change overnight if the bread winner loses their job or for that matter if the bread winner leaves a person and they have to bring up a family on their own. My heart goes out to the guy I witnessed throwing a brick through the window at the Job Centre premises and hearing him being totally inappropriate questions and expecting a person like him to find work with a broken arm it's unbelievably cruel. Then to watch him being led away by the police it totally upset me. The more I see the more I'm thankful for what I have but I know the feeling of desperation as I've been there myself too often.

Circumstances are different for all and when being faced with the same scenario you have to dust yourself down and try to move on the only way you know how. Today the spiritual church keeps me sane and gives me a sense of achieving something good in life.

When I delivered food parcels during the Christmas period for the needy it made me feel I was doing something purposeful especially to see their faces light

Up, with the gifts I'd brought. The joy it gives to know that the children will at least have food and will open a Christmas gift this year gives me that feeling of Christmas and lifts my spirits so much to be part of that I felt a sense of wellbeing.

On one occasion I called at a house with groceries I very large bright yellow melon was sat at the top of my basket. As soon as I got through the door one of the children called Joey eagerly approached me with a big smile on his face.

'Have you brought us a big yellow ball?' he asked me.

I was upset that the melon had not been a ball but also it's sad to think a child does not recognise or has never seen or tasted a fruit like a melon in his life.

After this four-year period of working at the Food Bank I have begun to move on to other things. These days I'm happy in my own company. I still do work for myself and charitable outlets but when I'm not working I enjoy walking and simply having a night in on my own with the lights down and find it therapeutic to sit quietly with candles lit and feel at peace.

The only irksome issue always is those damned Council Tax bills which are ongoing at the moment. I am feeling a little intimidated by the never-ending requests for money. My circumstances this year are financially less than I received last year. However, they keep persisting on sending me requests for a larger payment off me this year. How does that work?

When I feel driven to anger I turned to the art of meditation and having candles all around me is helping. Not sure I can get deep into it yet but I'm sure in time it will help me cope with anything that comes along.

CALM AND MOVING FORWARD

I felt things appeared to be progressing for the better to be honest, although I didn't want to tempt providence, in my experience trouble had always crept up on me, without reason or rhyme. I just prayed that good things may finally come my way. Making the best of life is what I've tried to achieve and I think I've made positive moves, attempting to deal with life in a different way. One thing for sure is that I can take a vacuum to bits and put it all back together. Something which comes in very handy since I've been trying my best to build a business in cleaning people's houses. Often their vacuums need emptying in order for me to do my job correctly. At least in this area I felt confident in tackling this type of job and the client is also happy that I saved them the job of doing it. It's all in a day's work for me and I truly enjoy get job satisfaction once I'd finished the cleaning and can see things sparkle.

Another thing I am determined to do is to try to stop smoking for good and all. It's hard, but I determined to succeed, this time, once my life becomes less stressful and I can see my way life moving forward in a much better light.

Just lighting candles or seeing a bunch of daffodils in a vase is something that makes me feel tranquil and trying to master the art of relaxation is a great part of my healing.

I suppose I'm allowed to have dreams though. I often walk pass the W H Smith's book shop in town, I day dream about me writing my own book and it being on sale. it gives me the strength to keep going and hopefully share my life with others who find themselves constantly worried about what would happen day in day out, always being consciously aware of the threats and the dangers around me. I am sure there are many out there who can connect to what has happened to me and relate to how I felt as a victim of other people who chose to abuse me in so many ways and can, perhaps, relate to what has happened to me. There is always a way out, never give up hope and more than anything you have to believe there is something or someone out there ready to help.

After that first day I'd braved it and entered the door of the Writers' Circle I now feel at home and was made to feel welcome. I feel it's doing me good to listen and learn about how to go about writing short stories and I'm slowly but surely feeling at home. They are a lovely bunch of people and I can't tell you how helpful they've been to me in me trying to achieve writing my own biography.

One of the exercises the writer's circles had challenged us all to write about, had been to write a short summary about one of the members of the group, only it had to be anonymous, so the class could decide who the person was at the end of reading each piece out in front of the class meeting. The only person I had got to know, a little, at that time was, Joyce, so I tried to make up a funny story.

I found it nerve racking reading it out, yet once I'd got through it everyone had a good laugh and it had made me feel included. This is another journey of learning for me and I enjoyed every minute of every meeting. To hear other people read of their experience has been great and a learning curve for me.

There are many types of book I've enjoyed and have been known to stay awake all night to finish them. Not a good idea when you have to get up for work though. I have read and enjoyed reading Martina Cole, Lesley Pearce and Colin Fry and many others including spiritual books, one written by a medium named Mia Dolan called 'The Gift' which I found fascinating and I would love to meet her in person. Her book certainly changed my way of thinking in a positive way.

Another escape for me when I hadn't to go to work or be at the charity shop I loved to walk for at least seven miles it made me feel free. I loved just getting out there up in the hills way above Burnley or over into Rossendale Clowbridge reservoir nothing beats the free fresh air and the remarkable scenery. I felt blessed to be fit and well enough to have climbed many hills and stood way out of sight of everyone just surveying the beauty of my surroundings. Something I intend to do, as it makes me feel alive, and I shall continue to do this for a very long time and have made it part of my daily routine.

Occasionally my friend Wendy would join me and we could go to further outlandish places like Hurstwood or climb the famous beauty spot Pendle Hill, with Wendy owing a car this was made possible. Even if it rained it was exhilarating and more often than not we'd get into some scrape or other. Like the time we got back to the car and found my friends' car had been wheel clamped or another time fell into a load of mud up to our necks then we were attacked by a vicious dog. It was for me a lot of fun and to be honest we laughed and laughed about it, a great dose of fresh air with good friends and laughter helped me overcome the bad things in life and a great part of healing.

We are still here to tell the tale but I don't believe I had ever come across a miserable walker along the way. Everyone said, good morning, good afternoon and sometimes it's good to have a chat. It's just the best feeling in the world.

In between all the many hats I wear I found the time to make jewellery with crystals which is a fulfilling spiritual hobby of mine. I once had an unusual rose quartz heart necklace which someone admired so much and thought it was beautiful it made me think that maybe I could make this sort of jewellery as a hobby and then sell it. It was offered to members and visitors of the spiritual church I attended and the money made from the proceeds was reinvested into buying more crystal but it is such a great hobby and one I loved to do.

Rose quartz is meant to heal emotional heartbreak, jokingly, in my case it gets very hot when I wear it. It's a wonder I get any made at all as I can't seem to sit still for more than ten minutes. There is also the fact they are nice gifts to make for friends and relations and almost all of them are surprised and thrilled with them.

Amongst other things I made bird houses, night lights, wax melts, Himalayan salts, lamp candles, oil burner, never a dull moment, I really don't know how I get through at times I try not to be down or bored and this is why I do so many activities to keep my mind alert in order to progress and move one. Going online and listening to the guided meditation which is hard to concentrate on but it is meditation is something I see as a challenge for me and it's something I look forward to mastering.

I would not be where I am now without the love and understanding I had received from the Spiritual Church and those beautiful people. I loved being a member and when I was nominated to become a member of the committee, which by the way came as a total surprise, I was pleased and happy to accept my responsibility to the church. It had made it possible for me to try to give back to others, who had graciously given their time and energy up in helping me, at a very difficult time in my life. I had needed their love and been given hope to get me through. It had given me the opportunity to give back to others who have given up their precious time to be there for me when I needed it the most.

LIFE TAKES A DRAMATIC TURN

So life is good I'd settled into a routine, I felt things were going well in my life. Regular visits to the spiritual church, and my social life couldn't have been going any better. I was relaxing more every day getting into a much more stable life and enjoying the silence when I'd felt I'd needed it. As well as that my sleeping pattern settled to a more constant and peaceful state, which I feel was due to self-meditation.

Recently, I'd been enjoying upgrading furniture and also finding items I could work on and turn them into useful items and I gained satisfaction and pleasure from this hobby. I made and recovered a footstool which sold for a small profit then I began to make clocks out of vinyl records, despite the fact at times I lost patience with the fiddly bits I often threw clock parts across the kitchen in a moment of frustration. I always persevered and finally managed to put the clock hands in the correct position. I smile when I think of the struggle yet I never gave up and successfully achieved my end goal.

At this time, in-between doing my jobs of work, I searched second hand shops and began looking for things to create or try to give an upgrade, and I was enjoying myself so much, life was good. I admit I developed a bad habit of snooping in skips when I was walking past them and just recently I saw a few wooden pallets discarded in it and decided to go back a little later to retrieve. To my utter dismay when I returned the skip had been collected. I was so upset about the thing I had planned in my mind to make them into Welsh type dressers. I almost cried but I just smiled and carried on with my quest.

My daughter Molly had turned 19 years old had decided to go to college and try to better herself and she managed to get interviewed and then given employment at an insurance office as a junior trainee, yet still be carrying on with her course work.

The weekend after the Manchester bombing she planned to go to a charity concert at Parklife held in Heaton Park in Manchester and was excited about it. Like most teenage girls she often had disputes with her friends over petty girly things. I'm certain most mothers with teenage daughters will say the same. Although at times girls can become truly awful with each other.

A few years earlier, whilst at junior school, Molly had returned home and told me one of her group of friends asked her how it felt not knowing who her father was. I was absolutely appalled to say the least how someone dared to say such a terrible thing to her at such a tender age. I could not retaliate or do much about it, though.

Molly did know who her father was and always had done; in fact, we all still got on well with her dad's sister at the time. Sadly, the contact between father and daughter was nonexistent. In my early days I had quite a temper on me and I've had to work hard on myself to remove this characteristic, though it isn't easy when you're surrounded by insensitive people. Putting that to one side I have to admit that Molly temperament was similar to mine. We never back away when confronted, especially in respect of an injustice.

On the day of the concert a row broke out during the day, prior to the event she and her friends were due to go to Parklife. The price of the festival ticket was seventy pounds and the girls who were with her refused to give Molly the ticket she had paid for.

This altercation carried on, not far from her home. In fact, it was getting a little out of hand as Molly had sent me a text message to ask me to come outside the house to help her and for me to see what had been going on.

As I stepped out of my gateway and looked downwards I could see one of the girls in the group, was waving a ticket in Molly's face. I could also see a male person in the back seat of the car. Molly lost it for a moment and moving towards her had grabbed her ticket, during the tussle the ticket had ripped.

The screaming and arguments carried on and as I didn't want to get into the middle of it all I'd persuaded Molly to back away from it and come back home with me. Molly was extremely upset about how these girls', who were supposed to be her closest friends, had been treating her. They had spent the whole of the afternoon bullying and mocking her and making her feel uncomfortable and anxious. I'd made us a brew, and she appeared to calm down a little.

After a while, Molly had decided to contact another friend of hers, who was also attending the same course at college with her. It had been arranged that, Molly would purchase another ticket on-line and treat her friend. They seemed to get on really well, her name is Olivia and apparently they'd hit it off right away and had become good friends. I'd already met Olivia and had found her to be a lovely well-mannered and a kind, friendly person.

Her new friend had agreed to collect her in her car. Whilst Molly waited for her to arrive she'd busied herself by blocking the lot of the bullying girls from snap chat and Face book. Her mind was made up she never wanted any further communication with any of them.

During the evening Molly had kept in touch with me, sending me messages letting me know they had arrived safely. Not long after this text message from Molly, I'd received a phone call from her. She had sounded very upset and told me as they entered Parklife they were told they were not admitting any more people after nine o'clock and that they had decided to make their way back home. They had arrived back about an hour later. Molly looked a little strange and her speech was racing at top speed she hardly stopped for breath.

Then Molly herself said she'd felt strange and to be honest she wasn't acting like herself at all. It was then she blurted out to us she felt certain those girls' had put something in her drink earlier that afternoon. She told me she had only had a cup of tea and bottle of orange during the day. I had hardly any time to absorb what she was saying as she turned and asked Olivia if she would take her to the hospital and before I knew what was happening they had left, leaving me feeling totally in shock.

Once I'd grasped the situation about what had just happened, I'd immediately sent Adam, my son a text message to come home quickly to take care of Darcy his younger sister so I could go to the hospital. I had to see Molly and find out what was going on, I was in bits with worry.

On my arrival at hospital I'd been greeted by a nurse who took me to see Molly, she was in a small cubical in A & E and was hysterical shouting and talking nonsense. I'd tried to tell the nursing staff as quickly as I could about what had happened throughout the day. I relayed to her the argument which had occurred and how violent it had become between Molly and her friends and that she had been treated badly by them all.

Most of the girls' that day had all had their faces professionally made up and for some reason one of the girls, in particular, told Molly she looked like a clown. When in fact, Molly had looked absolutely stunning, her makeup was beautiful. I was beside myself with worry and I couldn't believe anyone would ever do something like that to her, especially in a situation where they were supposed to be best friends. Molly has always been totally against drugs and very much a girl who enjoyed nothing better than sitting in with her boyfriend on a Saturday night at her Nana and Granddad's house. Drugs were alien to her. Although she was old enough to drink alcohol she had no liking for it. My mind was in a real state trying to go through it all in my mind.

Molly had continued in this state for five hours, rambling on so much so I had to leave and go into the car park where I completely broke down crying.

I couldn't comprehend what on earth had happened to my precious child as I stood there shaking and feeling utterly confused. This was a nightmare, having to watch her in such a dreadful state of distress. Finally, the nurse had come outside and had told me she thought I should go home and get some rest and they would ring when a bed became available.

I'd returned back into the hospital to let Molly know I was leaving to go home and that I would be back to see her in the morning. She'd screamed at me, accusing me of having left her to see those girls, outside in the waiting area. It was incredulous to me that she should be saying all this. It made absolutely no sense at all, and yet she seemed to be totally convinced those girls were there. Seeing the terror in her eyes I realized she was in a dreadful state and had been panicking. In her mind she'd believed the bullies were outside. I tried my best to explain I was alone and the girls were not at the hospital.

She'd become hysterical and told me to go. I'd felt utterly dumb struck, I'd turned and spoke with the nurse and then had phoned a taxi and gone home. I felt exhausted by the time I reached home and fell asleep instantly still holding on to my phone.

I'd awoken with a banging on the door and jumped up and there was a policeman at the door I ran down the stairs an opened door letting him inside. He'd then explained Molly had run away from the hospital over an hour and a half ago, and did they didn't have a photo of her? Adam was still here with me asleep in the living room, this was because we'd needed to be ready to return to the hospital if anything had happened to Molly. I'd explained to Adam that I would need to go with him.

Throwing a jacket on I'd rushed out of the house with the officer and began to search the length and breadth of Burnley, in the police vehicle. As I known, she was pretty much a home bird there was nowhere I could suggest we should look beyond the Burnley area. I explained briefly to the policeman what kind of a person Molly was and she was not a risk taker, she would never experiment with drugs at any point and had never smoked cigarettes as we carried on scouring the area around Burnley, sirens blaring and tearing through red traffic lights in and around the hospital and beyond.

Then it had occurred to me that Molly may have made her way to her sister's house as she had recently moved closer to where we lived. However, as they had fallen out over something earlier in the week I thought it would probably be the last place she would go. I immediately sent a text message to Katie my oldest daughter asking her not to say a word to Molly if she was there with her. Once we arrived at her home I went inside to find them both sat there drinking tea.

The policeman very patiently explained to Molly that the hospital had wanted her go back there and eventually she accepted she had to go but requested that the police officer came into the hospital with us, which he did. While we waited in a side room the policeman assured me he would be in touch the following day then after saying goodbye, he'd left.

From thereon in things went downhill, to be honest. Molly had been ranting on about people being there and when we looked around us we realized Molly was imagining this. She'd switched off her mobile phone and given it to me. That's when I knew for sure that something was terribly wrong. I mean, every teenager has their mobile phone welded to them and she was always on social media and snap chat etc.

We had waited several hours for a bed and finally a bed had been allocated and Molly had been transferred from Burnley General Hospital to the Royal Blackburn Hospital. When we arrived we realized Molly had been placed in a ward with quite a lot of old people. At this stage Molly was becoming aggressive, frustrated and talking utter rubbish I tried as hard as I could, along with the nursing staff to calm her down. She kept repeating the same thing over and over again about them so called friends saying things, it sometimes had made sense then other times it hadn't.

I hadn't known what to believe or what to think by this point, Kristen who is Molly's boyfriend had been with me at

106

that time and we were both bewildered by what we were seeing. Molly then began pushing and shoving and punching Kristen, by this time the ward was in an uproar. It must have been so frightening for all the patients and the nurses not knowing what to do to help her. Various medical tests were undertaken as the days passed, also a brain scan. As well as that they put a needle in spine for fluid, so many tests yet nothing appeared to be physically wrong.

As the day went on her behaviour became more bizarre she was writing lots of stuff down an acting really strange, myself and the others felt a little scared this was not Molly at all she was using swear words and it was awful to watch she lost bowel control. My friend Sarah was a God send, she was there by my side nearly every day and Kristen's' together with his dad Howard, his dad and Laura his step mum who I had not met before.

A few days later the mental health team had arrived at that time I thought they looked like three detectives they had asked me a few brief questions about Molly like 'had she acted this way before'. It was hard to answer a question like this because most parent who have teenager children will tell you there's plenty of rows, bad moods, sulks that's the way life is. Disagreements with people and misunderstandings are commonplace it's simply part of growing up.

She's no different from any other child and gets upset when family members fall out or getting pressure at work was also affecting her when she was made to feel like a total nobody and had been treated badly by a member of staff, who banged her cup on the desk every time she wanted Molly to get her another drink of tea or coffee?

What kind of individual does that to a young person? It is so hard at times for the younger generation today having to

107

trying to fit in. Having to be slim, own a smart mobile, have the best lipstick and also following ideas on the Instagram pages and loads of advice in magazines which are full of which diet to try.

Gone are the days when you would purchase a pound lipstick and a cheap perfume. It's all about having the latest this and that, expensive facials, being contoured up and filtered on a photo to look perfect or you are seen as a has been. I own two items of makeup my only vice is my obsession with eyebrows, never trust anyone with uncultured eyebrows is a favourite saying of mine.

After having spoken to the three members of the mental health team they'd gone to speak with Molly to ask her a few questions then had come to the decision to have her sectioned her under the mental health act for her own safety. That meant she's not allowed to leave for 27 days. Molly asked me later if I would take her for a walk in the grounds and no sooner had we got outside I realized she had tricked me as tried to run away.

It took seven nurses to catch up with her she ran like the wind. It turned out that she only wanted an ice lolly from the canteen. The nurses had been kind and understanding. It's obviously their responsibility to look after Molly and obviously they've been specially trained. They'd know what to do and they did a wonderful job. At all times they were aware of how poorly Molly was and to be put on this particular special ward, had not been the best place for a person like Molly who is suffering with psychosis behaviour and should have been detained.

Molly was constantly shouting and screaming, she never slept for days on end and there was no explanation for this and apparently no bed had been available on a mental health ward. It took a week for them to find her a special care place. During her week's stay there she ran myself and the nursing staff ragged. She ticked every meal on menu request forms and the gluten free diet. She pushed the nurses, ripped hospital notes I'd never witness this kind of behavior from her in my entire life.

Finally, they'd managed to get a member of the hospital staff called Graham to sit with us for two hours. He was an exceptionally lovely man and whilst he had sat for a while with Molly myself and Kristen, (Molly's boyfriend) had gone for something to eat. Whenever I left Molly she would shout at us to *'fuck off'* it was absolutely heartbreaking.

Many nights after being at Molly's bedside all day I couldn't sleep because of the worry and the first thing on my mind in a morning was to immediately ring the hospital to see what kind of night she'd had.

BURNLEY GENERAL HOSPITAL

After the longest week of my life I'd made regular phone call to speak with the nurse and she had informed me they had finally secured a bed for Molly and she'd be returned back to the General Hospital in Burnley, We were informed that this would be a secured ward, where she'd be safe.

I'd arranged to go at 11am in morning and I had dreaded the thought of seeing my beautiful daughter having been placed into the secure wing of the hospital. Adam, my son had already left for a planned holiday to Greece. He was truly unhappy about leaving me and Molly behind but I insisted he needed a holiday.

On arrival at the ward I was a little scared and in shock to the core, never would I have imagined in a million years Molly would be in such a place as this. The nurses had let me in and the doors were immediately locked behind me. There was a large table and a designated drinks area then the bedrooms. This was an assessment ward so the behaviour of patients can be assessed by the staff every fifteen minutes.

To my horror, I had stared incredulously at my daughter, unable to take in what she was doing. She had been moving up and down the ward picking up anything she could lay her hands on. Rubbish, bin litter and everything and anything she could possibly lay her hands on. She'd thrown mattresses off the beds and had been behaving aggressively towards staff and the patients it seemed as if she was possessed. I honestly could not believe this was my child, my normally quiet and sensible child. 'Who in God's name had turned her into this unrecognizable psychotic lunatic?' I'd felt like I was breaking down at witnessing her behaviour and had struggled not to let her see my tears flow.

110

Over the next few weeks I taken many things for her to the hospital toothbrushes, pyjamas, clothes and just the things which Molly would need in hospital to make her feel clean and presentable. The next time I would visit all the stuff I'd taken in had been given away or taken from her. I'd often walk on to the ward and see one of the patients walking past me wearing one of the jumper and pajamas, which I had left for Molly.

Day after day had been a nightmare, I never known what to expect once I got there. One day I was taking a phone call when I was informed Molly was on a table smashing the roof up and seven members of the staff had to get her down. The nurses had no alternative but to give her an injection to sedate her.

I was informed the strength of the medicine had enough strength in it to knock a horse out. Two hours later Molly was up and at it. She had her polar bear called Snowbell, everyone knew snowbell, a teddy she's had since she's was a small child. She kept saying really strange stuff the nurse told me. She said it was as if her mind was going five times faster than it should be, she still hadn't been sleeping either.

Anyone who has ever witnessed a person with psychosis could understand what I am saying. People suffering with this often see things which are not there to a normal person, to the patient it is perfectly true they actually are seeing the things and suffering terrifying side effects. Like a fear of entering a bathroom, feeling paranoid that the nurses are the enemy and they hit out at them it's very upsetting. Their hearing becomes hypersensitive and they find they can hear

111

conversations on the ward which seem extremely loud to Molly. That possibly upset her more than anything else. Another of her extreme behaviour was when one of the other patients was in a wheelchair and Molly believed the girl could walk and tried to pull her out of the chair to help her walk.

At other times she had got on well with some of the people and yet for some reason disliked others who were on that ward. It was suggested, to me, I should keep my visits short for a while to see if it would be more beneficial for Molly. Yet Molly had become more aggressive, she'd scream and was banging on the doors to come out with me. It was truly awful. I'd sit outside on the hospital steps and weep my heart out, having had to see her acting and behaving so out of character. It was clear to me Molly was an extremely poorly girl and she wasn't getting any better.

I'd carried on ringing every 3 hours and by now I knew most of the nurses and was told they were giving her an anti-psychotic drug and benzos, yet they were having little or not much effect. At that stage we were still not sure if it was the fact her drink had been spiked, or if she was suffering from paranoid thoughts because of the way her so called friends had been treating her.

It must have been totally terrifying for Molly to find herself hearing voices, to her these were voices were real. There was no explanation for why she suddenly started talking utter rubbish and stuffing all kinds of items down her top and pants. Practically anything she could find. It's a wonder I didn't go under throughout this painful time. I often returned home and passed out with having to cope with the constant episodes she was going through, I was having to see with my own eyes. It was torture I'd hated to see her suffering and eventually I could feel myself going into a decline I lacked energy I felt I was going through hell with no way out. My whole body was draining away into a state of collapse.

I'd rung up one morning to see what her night had been like and they'd said don't be alarmed when you see Molly's hair. She has been back combing it and has pushed, straws, paper and pens a total of thirty-four items sticking out even some toast in there. On our arrival we entered and there she had been looking like a crazy cat walk model, her face was orange, she had obviously helped herself to someone's makeup she insisted she was a Umpah Lumpah and I've had to agree there was a likeness. I asked her to wipe her face, also the drawings she done on her arms and body. She absolutely would not allow anyone near her hair. It was now consisting of Vimto apple juice and paper glue I have never seen anything like it!

After two more days had passed I insisted that Sarah and I were coming back that night to wash it. It took both of us hours. We needed to use six bottles of conditioner, to be able to comb through it a little. Sadly we also needed to use the scissors to cut away some parts of the mess. Followed by a great deal of hair oil and gently managed to get a comb through it. What a mess it was not to mention how painful it had been for Molly, she was in agony whilst we struggled to free all the debris from what used to be her shining glory, her beautiful hair. It made me upset to have to be the one to inflict this pain and I can't explain how upset I was it's the worst thing I've had to do my whole life.

Of course we were on first name speaking terms with all the nurses and I'd felt able to voice my concerns and listen to what they were saying as well. I couldn't believe how long Molly had been hospitalized and there didn't appear to be much improvement to me. When I wasn't on the phone to the hospital I was on the ward giving Molly support. I was worried sick by the things Molly was saying was she was still making no sense what-so-ever. All we knew for sure at that time was that Molly was suffering from psychosis. It's a severe mental condition with shattered emotions and losing touch with reality. They see things that don't exist and they can hear voices. It really is frightening for everyone. Molly was like a lost soul and no longer behaving like the Molly we all loved. Days went by in a blur and her behavior worsened. She took an instant dislike to a certain nurse who had a tirade of verbal abuse thrown at her by Molly. A few of the nurses were punched and kicked, one having to go to another department to get her arm looked at it was truly awful.

I, myself was pushed and squeezed a few times, by Molly. Adam, who had his work badge around his neck, had it tugged hard and had to restrain her from chocking him. At that time, she'd kept talking a total load of rubbish, which was illegible whilst her mind was going off like an express train her speech quickening up to five times faster than an ordinary person. She wouldn't go to the toilet alone and I'm sure the other patients were a bit wary of her. It took seven nurses to pin her down several times to contain her. She carried her polar bear round with her everywhere the one she called Snowbell.

I arrived one night at hospital with my friend Sarah to see the disabled girl from the ward outside with Snowbell on her knee inside a sock she informed me Molly had said take the polar bear outside for some fresh air, it really was bizarre she paced around the ward out of touch with reality sometimes writing down car number plates. We still didn't know much at all. All we could do was to put our trust in these dedicated nurses and they were truly all brilliant. One day I arrived at the ward and we all sang like Whitney Houston I actually felt at home there, sometimes there has to be something to lighten the day and put a smile on your face on that ward.

I spoke with two of the nurses. Molly called one of them Jenny because she looked like her college teacher, her real name was Lisa she always went out of her way to talk to us. It really was very confusing at times for me to cope with and for Molly to be going through so much distress. I cried many times on my departure from the secure ward by now Molly was on her medication an anti-psychotic drug but like everything it takes time they was reluctant to put her on her it in first place because of her age they couldn't say if it was the start of something like bipolar or a one off psychosis episode. They just had to try a get the medication right she was not sleeping and was very aggressive it was never-ending.

During this time she was placing items in her bra and lifting her top up she didn't know if her boyfriend was Adam at times it was very upsetting and rambling a right load of non-sensible words. I couldn't see an end to it although we tried to keep some normality when we visited Molly. We tried to interest her in playing dice. Adam and Molly were guessing what number it would land on and Molly shouted 7 Adam burst out laughing and she whizzed the dice straight at his forehead telling us both to *fuck off*. When I asked her if she knew where she was she had no idea whether it was night or day.

The following day when I'd left the ward she'd banged on the door for an hour screaming. I watched from the darkness of the car park and cried alone. My nightly phone calls with the nurses kept me going they put my mind at rest as the days wore on there was little or no improvement the voices got louder in Molly's head the noise of the ward was making her worse. She had also had several rows with other patients, all of them suffering with mental issues themselves. As she was only in there for a mental health assessment she continued to be extremely unwell and possibly had by this time had more fights than Amir Khan. One day she asked me why everyone was scared, I'd laughed she really didn't have any idea of what she had done whilst being in there.

 I'd questioned my faith many times I asked myself 'Why has this happened' I cried! I tested my close friends and told them how I felt no-one who knew my family and Molly well, couldn't believe what had happened to her. I felt really sorry for myself and Kristen, Molly's boyfriend and during this time we often laughed and cried together it has definitely made our bond stronger. He's been there throughout all the terrible times and has more than proved to me what a top person he is. Once again my close friends were also there giving me support.

Father's Day had come and gone. There were presents in Molly's bedroom at home still wrapped for her granddad. Molly had always put so much time into buying gifts and had them ready well before the date intended. It felt like the family had been split in two. Life without Molly in it had been too much for all of us to bear. We all missed her so much. Darcy, Molly's little sister was unable to visit the hospital because you had to be 18 to go on ward. She had, therefore, written a little note for Molly, which Sarah and I were to deliver, together with fruit and other small gifts which we thought may help to occupy Molly and help her settle to something. It was hard though, as she couldn't sit still for long and talked incessantly, most of what she said was illogical and gibberish, which made no sense at all. For some strange reason Molly had taken a liking to one of the other patient who was from Zimbabwe. The name Molly used to call her was Seeboo. She'd sat with her all the time and would stroke her head. Seeboo was very quiet she never spoke apart from saying the words - 'Help me, my light has gone out am I going to die.' Other than that she stayed silent, not that she could get a word in edgeways with Molly who was talking none stop nonsense.

One night on my arrival at hospital the nurses took me aside and we went in a room and they informed me Molly was being transferred to Bradford Hospital, a private hospital because the ward was too busy and it wasn't helping Molly recover. They feared for her safety and their own. I openly wept. I wouldn't be able to get to Bradford it was going from bad to worse. I returned home from my visit distraught. They would not be telling Molly until it was time to go the nurse assured me it was for the best.

THE BRADFORD PRIVATE CLINIC

It took a while for me to accept that at some point, even as I sat her at home, that she would travel to Bradford alone without me to comfort her. Later on that night I received a phone call from the Burnley General. I was told that even though Molly had been a handful to deal with they had all grown to like her, which is what most people always say about Molly, she was such a likeable person before all this happened her. The nurse I was speaking to asked me to please keep in touch and let them all know if Molly health improves. I could only pray that one day soon, I and Molly would return to see them and show them how sweet a girl she is once she is well again.

It had felt strangely odd to me to not be getting up-dates from the nursing staff during the evenings, something I'd become used to. Whilst having chats with the nurses in Burnley on more than one occasion it had been explained to me that approximately 1 in 4 people will experience a mental health problem each year in the United Kingdom and 70 million workdays are lost due to mental illness including anxiety, depression and stress related conditions. One in ten young people have a clinical mental health disorder diagnosed. With all the government cuts there aren't enough beds. Almost 6,000 mental health patients are sent out of the area for care it's simply not adequate and should not be happening. These patients need continuing care and be allowed to have a daily visit from their close family, especially when the patient is in their teenage years, they should have their family by their side whilst suffering from mental health problems.

My constant worry at that moment was that Molly would be so shocked to find herself so far away in a strange environment which would be alien to her. She knew all the nurses in Burnley and she would feel, for certain, totally out of her depth I felt it would certainly be detrimental to her state of mind. Not to mention that it caused me a great deal of distress too not knowing how she was feeling. For all the family this caused them and me to fear for her safety and possibly the worst thing to have happened to Molly.

I was told the following day that Molly had finally been collected at something like 2am in the morning and taken overnight to her new hospital bed in Bradford. The minute I awoke I rang to ask the nurse at for the number of the Bradford hospital and was alarmed to find out they didn't have a contact number.

Molly had left her handbag on the ward at Burnley she had taken nothing with her only Snowbell, her bear. It made me so upset on hearing this, it made things even worse as far as I was concerned. The question in my mind is: '*Was she taken out of the ward screaming and kicking into the ambulance.*' My mind was in such a state I needed that number I needed to speak to someone to reassure me that she was okay.

Once I had found the number for Bradford I called straight away. All I got was being told was '*can you ring back in an hour's time.*' When I did ring back I was fobbed off time and time again. Eventually I insisted on speaking to someone and finally I was put through to someone in charge who informed me Molly was fine apart from launching her slippers at someone's face and had also punched a nurse in the face and had burst her lip.

The only information forthcoming about how Molly herself was in respect of had she been seen etc. Finally, I was told that she had been seen by two doctors and the nurse informed me her medication had been increased and they can only hope for an improvement.

I chatted with the nurse and arranged to visit the following Sunday. They work on an appointment system so I had to make a booking so I made an appointment. I could only pray we see an improvement in her after not seeing her for all most a week.

Molly would be celebrating her twentieth birthday next month and I couldn't wait for her to open the lovely gifts I had bought for her. I had found her some lovely pajamas and also I found a gorgeous unicorn teddy bear a friend for Snowbell. Like Molly had said to me on a recent visit *'Snowbell has seen a lot of life hasn't he?'* so I thought she would be pleased to receive another teddy to hug.

I found it hard waiting and hoping every minute of every day that sooner or later we would be able to bring Molly back home to us.

I continue to work with a heavy heart and every hour I think about my daughter and just try to stay positive and believe there will be an improvement by the time I see her again.

It was doubly hard for me to get any feedback from Bradford at all. I would be fobbed off time and time again; no-one would speak to me. I became extremely angry and upset not knowing what my girl was doing and if she was getting any better but absolutely no-one would come to the phone. On most days I remember counting sixteen phone calls.

Every day I could not get a reply what-so-ever. I was getting more and more stressed to say the least but there was no other way for me to find anything out about how Molly was. This went on for day after day it seems once a person is sectioned the parents have no rights at all about treatments or care of the person you had handed them over too it is against all your human rights as far as I was concerned. She is my daughter and I love her so much it broke my heart over and over again.

Once Molly was coping better she started to phone me from the ward telephone. To be fair a lot of the time Molly didn't make much sense but to be honest it was just lovely to hear her voice. I lived for these phone calls often breaking down in floods of tears afterwards. I was still unable to sleep at night and lived on my e-cig and coffee to get me through my work but couldn't lift my spirits at all. I tried to keep strong yet everywhere I looked I saw teenage girls living their lives and enjoying themselves and I thought that is what my Molly should be doing not being placed in an imprisoned environment with people who must seem odd to her even though she's ill herself there were others in there so much worse than she was.

I was so low I'm afraid I'm beginning to lose my faith in the church which had always carried me through all the awful things I'd had in my life. Today however, I feel so wronged by life and would say often to myself or even God if he was listening. 'What did I ever do to deserve such a pain and suffering in respect of my children and my life as a whole?'

I just couldn't come to terms with what had happened to me, or for that matter what this had done to our family as a whole. These past weeks have torn me apart it has been unbearable at times.

You'd think by now I should be used to coping with life as it hasn't been an easy one but I never complain I keep on going and doing what I can, I cannot let my daughter down after all the weeks of torment she's been through.

Again it never rains but it pours. A dear friend of mine was battling against drug addiction and yet managed to pull herself away, kept strong and immediately went back into a programme by going to back to regular drug addiction meetings. I felt her strength we've been through a lot throughout our lives and always support one another throughout any trials and hardships. It's not easy pulling yourself out of a crisis but somehow or another our friendship and support makes us find the strength from within to fight back and come through whatever it is.

I had counted the days down to Sunday it was Molly's birthday on the Tuesday. So, Myself, Kristen (Molly's boyfriend) and Adam, my son set off to Bradford armed with get well cards, messages and a few treats and presents for her. On arrival we entered the building and we were immediately instructed to place any mobile devices in a locker it felt like a prison. Then the official went ahead and searched everything we had brought for Molly spreading it all out on the floor in reception.

We were taken to a room with three members of staff and when I saw Molly sat there looking so forlorn I wanted to run over to her and give her a big hug and a kiss her but we were told we were not allowed to go near her. We couldn't even offer her a drink from one of the drinks we had on us due to the fact the top having been opened prior to entering the hospital.

Molly looked totally absent and had obviously been well sedated and looked wax like, her face relaxed and calm with no recognition of us being there. She sat there drugged up sitting on the floor and moving a small toy car around.

It felt so wrong to me, one of the staff members, Steve made a bit of chit chat none of them were in a uniform it seemed odd. I had a bad feeling about this place if I am honest, the visit went too quickly as far as we were concerned, so sadly we had to leave and head back to our home. Mind you, with my son, Adam doing the driving it was much quicker as we went around the bends we had to hang on for dear life.

We could only go Sunday due to family work schedules and it wasn't that easy with it being in Bradford, we all had to work to keep the roof over our heads. Kristen and his dad, Howard and step mum Laura were very supportive on a few occasions they were able to go over to see Molly and of course we kept in touch via emails and text messages. They are all lovely people and caring it's possibly brought our two families closer together.

Of course, I still kept up my regular pointless phone calls to Bradford and received plenty of phone calls from Molly; sometimes she talked utter rubbish and regularly put other patients on phone to chat to me. One of the patients pleaded with me to please, please, help us get us out of here. I felt When I arrived home I went on the internet and looked up this hospital on the internet and was totally shocked to find out a patient was killed by another patient and had smothered the person with a pillow. This only made me feel I was right about that place it didn't seem right for such a young and emotional girl to be kept there in my opinion.

This only added to my constant worry on a daily basis I felt there was no hope left for her if she were to stay there much longer. I had little faith and I saw no hope what-so-ever. The only joy for me was to hear my phone ring and see the call was from Molly. It seemed a little bizarre to me and the calls were at random times, and though her conversations often made little sense at all it made me feel so useless with not being able to get her away from there. She often cried when she called me and I was too choked up at times to speak to her without breaking down. It's a terrible experience to go through knowing that's your daughter there and you can't even take her in your arms and make her feel loved that has got to be wrong not having physical contact with hugs from her family.

I'd be at home making meals on auto pilot and wishing time away so I could be with her. Molly rang one day her voice was slowed up and she sounded drugged up. Then I heard screaming and alarms going off in the background, Molly had just dropped the phone and I imagined it dropping mid-air. The sirens rang out loud for a good ten minutes then the phone went dead.

Imagine what was going through my mind at this stage, I tried my best to ring back but as usual there was no reply. I tried and tried feeling weak and powerless until finally I got through to a person who spoke very little English. I gave her my name my daughter's name and the ward name but he couldn't understand a word. I then said can you get a nurse to speak with me and yet again was told to ring later by this point I was hysterical.

I'd been helping out at the charity shop in the back room at this point when the phone rang and it was from a social worker who had gone to visit Molly. His name was Patrick. I spoke to him for a short while he told me he'd seen scratches on Molly's face and had immediately requested some medical attention. I talked to him about my concerns and said in no uncertain terms I want Molly out of there as soon as possible. He assured me he would try his best it had been costing five thousand pounds a week to be kept in this private hospital which was picked up by the NHS because of their being no general hospital beds available.

It's shocking the system is failing miserably more patients are sent hundreds of miles away for care due to a shortage of beds more than 5,400 mental health patients had to travel out of area for a psychiatric bed last year. Some patients are being sent almost 300 miles away due to local units being full more than 90 percent out of area placements due to bed shortages. The whole matter needs assistance and more funding it's a sorry state of affairs people with mental health issues deserve better it feels like a breach of people's human right.

Community services are being stripped back there's more pressure on acute services the funding isn't enough and are not functioning properly its unacceptable that many patients are receiving care so far from home I was assured by Patrick, the social worker, who told me that they were having to wait for a bed in a NHS hospital and as soon as one became available again Molly would be placed somewhere closer to her home.

The week flew by as we arranged to take Molly's sister who is 13 years old to see her sister and had booked the correct appointment then off we set to Bradford armed with treats sealed in the packs, birthday cards etc. We had got within a mile of the hospital when I received a phone call from Bradford hospital saying the visit was cancelled due to Molly kicking off and had attacked a staff member.

We were torn apart, never in all her 19 years, had we ever spent a birthday apart Darcy was really upset we all were. Once we arrived I insisted on speaking to a nurse which I was refused. I started to lose my temper or my mind I can't decide which as I repeatedly demanded a nurse come down and I also said in no uncertain terms that I wanted an explanation too! I was so sick of being fobbed off by the staff members here.

Finally a nurse arrived to see me. Her face was badly scratched and I began to think she must be the nurse who had been assaulted by Molly. It soon became clear to me that Molly had behaved badly and they needed to discipline her by not allowing her to see us. Sad but true I'm afraid. Nevertheless we left feeling deflated and worried for Molly.

I kept a record of everything and wrote it down on my calendar. Another week goes by I was told nothing at all about Molly wellbeing. Every time Molly rang me she sounded calm but heavily drugged. On certain occasion, if I was lucky, Steve the only nurse I felt relieved to speak to as he understood my concern, in respect of Molly's treatments, and obviously my need to know how she was. When Steve picked up the phone, he always had the time to give me at least some information of what Molly was doing and all about what medications she was on. Although it was understandable it was extremely worrying for me, it made a difference that at least one person in there helped me and I was so grateful to him.

I think I had been a little spoilt by the nurses who work at the NHS hospitals as they never minded me calling to speak to them to put my mind at rest, maybe I shouldn't be saying this, but it was a real lifeline to me and made a big difference in making me feel better. They were all lovely and caring nurses I've ever had the pleasure to meet. All put my mind at ease and understood how they would feel had it been a daughter of theirs. Whereas Bradford, had no time at all to speak with me on one occasion one of the doctors from there rang me to say in a laid-back tone, quote: –

'Yeah, she will be back at work next week'

I thought he needs help if you ask me. They were still giving Molly anti-psychotic drugs once a week. Patrick the social worker didn't seem happy about this, I believed the doctor from Bradford acted very unprofessionally by not speaking to me privately instead of talking to me when Molly was in the room. I could hear her in the background she was far from improving as far as I was concerned.

THE HARBOUR MENTAL HOSPITAL BLACKPOOL

Again, we got a phone call telling us Molly would be leaving in two hours' time as a bed had been found in an NHS hospital in Blackpool called 'The Harbour' a two-year-old hospital. There are 154 mental health beds in the Harbour and I felt overjoyed when I got there to see at last she was in a six bed ward and her care was of a much higher standard. Three members of staff had travelled with her by car from Bradford to Blackpool I felt so relieved at last I thought all the family will be able to visit her in Blackpool which could only be a good sign to all of us.

I have to admit I did feel slightly nervous on my first visit to The Harbour and prepared myself thinking I may be faced with lots of people running around in all states of mental state of health. Instead I was surprised to see it was silent and more peaceful as and it was clearly a very well-run department. I felt at relaxed right away though I did feel sad for those people with mental problems left behind in Bradford hospital and are unlikely to get out of there but as far as Molly is concerned I felt she was beginning to receive the best care she could possibly get. Though I must admit I still miss the nursing staff in the Burnley.

I looked forward to the next visit and again prepared myself for seeing lots mentally ill people running around the ward as I had previously witness but it was, by contrast, peaceful and quiet and an extremely well run hospital even the reception staff were pleasant and helpful. Something which I'd not experienced at other establishments Molly had been in. I felt at as at ease straight way well, as at peace as I much as I could be, when visiting a mental health ward.

Molly seemed much better but still a long way off being herself, the Molly we knew and loved so much. After spending two weeks at The Harbour Mental Health Unit, Molly was once again returned to our home town in Burnley.

I was pleased to be having her nearer to me because travelling over to Blackpool and Bradford had been difficult in respect of transport and to have to rely on friends and my son Adam to take me but these had to be mostly evening visits. I would have loved to have visited Molly on a daily basis but for me, it hadn't been an option. I had needed to work to keep the roof over our heads as well as having to be there for my thirteen-year-old daughter, Darcy. Of course it may have been an option for me to get on a bus or train, yet Bradford hospital is not easy to get to and the extra time it would take to get on a bus or train to Bradford or Blackpool would not have allowed me very much time to spend with Molly.

Throughout this worrying time I would be in touch with Molly by phone, I bought her a 'pay as you go' phone for her to speak to me daily, she had no desire to have her own mobile phone back to her once she had passed it to me and she never asked for it again.

A dear friend, Carrie spent all her spare time to help me out. Apart from Adam and of course Kristen, Molly's childhood sweetheart, and his family visited in the evening regularly and this was so appreciated. I felt thankful to have such constant support from everyone. My mum and dad obviously were my strength too. Molly is very close to them they miss her terribly not seeing her popping her head around the door everyday a she always does with a happy smile on her face. She loves them so much it breaks my heart to see her looking sad and alone most of the time on visits.

BACK TO BURNLEY GENERAL HOSPITAL

I did feel I could see a slight improvement once she returned to Burnley. There was a meeting arranged at the Burnley General to discuss Molly's case. I went along to meet up with Patrick, her social worker, a consultant psychiatrist at the hospital and her nurse from the mental health ward in Burnley. The psychiatrist began to ask Molly a few questions. He began by asking Molly about whether she could hear voices in her head as she had previously experienced, to which she told them she didn't hear voices. They also asked her at this time if she had ever felt suicidal. Again Molly told them she did not feel suicidal.

Following on from this meeting it was decided that Molly could now begin to spend time at home with me and the family but she had to return back to the ward at night because she had been prescribed a new medication and needed to be monitored.

I felt strongly that it would be too much of an ordeal for Molly coming home so suddenly, after all she'd pretty much been from pillar to post over a period of eight to thirteen weeks at different mental institutions. When she had been sent to Bradford, because of the lack of beds anywhere else, she asked during her time there if she was in prison. I have mentioned earlier how awful the experience had been for Molly.

Whilst spending time there in the Bradford clinic and not seeing anyone during the week because of the distance and also the strict appointment system they had in place we always had to adhere to those rules. I feel it was not in Molly's best interests to be in that place. I am her mum. I know my child and I know by visiting her and speaking to her daily by phone I knew in my heart that

Molly would not be able to cope with the outside world instantly. I wanted her home, make no mistake, I love her with all my heart but I have a mother's instincts and I knew it would take a long while before Molly would return to being Molly again.

Despite my concerns Patrick, her social worker seemed determined to have her discharged. I felt sure this would not be the correct decision but I had to go along with what I was being told. On her daily visits home she seemed fine yet quiet. Molly stayed awake during the day whilst she stayed next door with her adored grandma and granddad as I needed to work. We had a meal together at night with all the family around her, Kristen, Molly's boyfriend, her sister Darcy and Adam her brother.

It was a few days later when Molly asked me if she could return to the hospital early, she said she felt funny, ill. Her granddad immediately got us into the car and we took her to the hospital as quickly as we could.

We were informed by the nurse at Burnley General hospital she would call the doctor out. We waited for an hour or so but he didn't arrive. We had no choice but to return home leaving Molly behind with the nursing staff.

My dad returned the following morning to collect Molly for the day and was informed the doctor had only just visited her. I wanted Molly to be safe and well on the new medication she was on it was called Zopiclone as well as taking 2grms of Temazepam. I was getting increasingly worried that Molly may relapse and go backwards and experience psychotic episode like she had previously suffered. This would have been catastrophic for Molly because if they decided she needed to be returned to the hospital, at this time she would automatically have lost her bed place at the Burnley General hospital and could end up being sent off somewhere else anywhere in the country. This was the situation at the present time and I had begged and pleaded with her social worker Patrick to change his opinion about sending her home in the first place.

There is always a shortage of beds for people in need of help. I've seen and heard so much about the needs of those in mental institutions and feel sad for all those having to be sent away from home and even then they only have the basic amount of things to wear, sleep in etc. Unless they are lucky enough to have family members to supply such things, in many cases they have no visitors at all. The things we all take for granted, like toothpaste, toiletries, underwear to mention but a few of what they lack. I understood more after realising why some of these sad looking people would steal clothes off Molly whilst being sectioned at the Burnley hospital.

It was decided that Molly would come home with my dad and the social worker Patrick who informed him would get some support in place for Molly from the mental health team and hopefully arrange a meeting with the mental team at Molly's own home.

Somehow I could not get the message through to anyone that Molly's needs were, in effect, urgent. A week is a long time to wait for somebody to give her the help she needed now. I was accused by Patrick of not wanting Molly at home. I cried with frustration. I desperately wanted Molly back home but I knew she needs much more professional help than our family were able to give her in respect to the correct medication she should be taking.

Patrick had even asked Molly if she would like him to find her a flat to live in on her own. At this stage Molly was incapable of making any decisions due to her mental state and to have been asked by Patrick, if she wanted to go to a flat on her own, not only was this a ludicrous thing to have said to Molly, it was exceedingly insensitive of him. All it did was to throw Molly into an increased state of anxiety and confusion. All I could do was to hold Molly tight and try to reassure her. I should not have been placed in this impossible position.

This state of affairs sent me into total panic mode. He didn't seem to understand my concerns. It was like trying to get through to a brick wall. Although, I imagine he had received training to be a social worker, in my opinion, he was in no way qualified to make a diagnosis or decision with relating to what Molly should be told. She was extremely vulnerable and confused and not capable of thinking for herself. What on earth did he think he was talking about? He was not a qualified psychiatrist? Neither am I, but I knew he shouldn't be saying things like this to Molly in the state she was in.

It took me a long while to comfort her after I'd spoken to him. I explained that I was doing my best and I certainly wanted her, more than anything, back home with us all but only when she showed she was ready. She was very tearful and so was I. To make her totally feel like I wanted her close she slept with me every night from then on.

So, the meeting was set for the following week. Prior to that Molly had an electro cardiac graph done, her pulse rate was 145 which was high according to the doctor but he said he would arrange an appointment for her to be checked out.

MOLLY IS DISCHARGED HOME

It was the May Bank Holiday weekend but it was still early days for Molly being at home with us. As it had been Kristen twenty first birthday that weekend, he naturally wanted to celebrate with friends and Molly, of course. Molly was simply not in any fit state to be partying, she looked tired and to be honest you never get much sleep in a hospital, all she seemed to do is sleep. She hadn't even unpacked her things, yet.

Her Granddad had taken Molly into town on the Saturday morning so she could buy a present for Kristen. She didn't look well at all and when she got home it was obvious that there was something the matter with her. We decided to return to the hospital to have her checked out. After waiting in casualty for three hours they gave her another ECG. Molly mentioned her heart felt to be beating very fast in her chest. It could have been a panic attack but we needed her to be examined. After the ECG her heart rate was still the same. It took hours of sitting there waiting for her to come through. Finally, we were told they couldn't find her file but discharged her. So off we went and took her home.

That night, I cuddled close to Molly in my bed and prayed to God things would soon get better for her.

Molly's social worker, Patrick came out to see her the following day. All Molly did was beg him none stop to help her she told him she didn't feel right. It was just three days before a meeting would take place on the Thursday at my mum's house with the social worker and the consultant.

All Molly did since returning home with me was to sleep apart from coming down for her meals then returned to bed, she told me she only felt better when she was lying down. It was awful for me to witness. I was in bits about what to do for her.

I'd kept myself busy to stop me going mad, I spent time logging into my phone and catching up on mail and then set about making tables out of old pallets, lamps from old gin bottles and also I had recently bought a very old 80s caravan and was trying to get it looking better.

I did think once Molly was feeling stronger it would be something we could do up together and keep her occupied by make pretty seating and cushions. It would be a project for mother and daughter and I look forward to that very much. I was dreaming of a time life would return to normal and we could all be a true family again.

It has seemed a lifetime of suffering for Molly over the last thirteen weeks, a total nightmare if I'm honest I kept thinking '*come on we're going to get through this Molly*' I have always been strong and purposeful and fight with every core of my being, but when faced with what had happened to Molly, all the ups and the downs, I have to admit I was feeling extremely depressed underneath but have to keep up appearances for everyone, especially my youngest daughter Darcy, it's been hard on her and I've not been giving her as much attention recently because time just hasn't allowed us that special mum/daughter time, but she's a loving a kind girl and understands. It's been hard for her it's been hard for all of us right now.

The day following the bank holiday the social worker called to say the meeting had been set for Thursday which I already knew of course. My good friend Carrie and had sent me a text message later and had asked me if I would go and see her new house.

Molly was upstairs fast asleep and I did feel like the walls were coming in on me having been home all the time so I agreed to go and look. My dad was right outside our door painting his fence so I knew Molly would be fine as they are vigilant where Molly is concerned. So when I contacted dad to check on Molly he told my mum had just been in the house around 4.30pm to check on her she'd told him Molly was up and having a bath and had shouted down to mum that she was fine and getting ready to come down.

I arrived home at 5.30pm, when I had expected Darcy back home, after spending the bank holiday weekend with her dad. I put the key in the lock and opened the door, stepped into the hallway and turned to shut the door. I glanced up the stairway and in my mind's eye believed I saw Molly at the top of the stairs coming down, when I looked again to my horror she was hanging from the staircase with a sports bag strap around her neck.

I screamed hysterically, knowing in my heart what had happened but in total utter disbelief. I dashed next door my dad almost had a heart attack as I screamed so loudly. I can't even remember what I said I only remember we went back into my home and together lifted Molly down from where she was hanging. She still felt warm and I made myself believe we could bring her back.

Frantically I tried to ring for an ambulance but in the end I had thrown down the phone, and dad and I had tried everything we could to resuscitate Molly, but it was too late, she had died.

It's hard to recall the order of how things evolved, being in total shock. I had been totally unable to think straight. Yet I must have sent Adam a text message. All I can remember is Adam, my son arrived about the same time as the ambulance, and then I remember a police car had arrived.

I had knelt down and hugged and kissed Molly and wept, there was nothing we could have done to save her. I couldn't believe she would have given us all of this pain I was beyond grief. I kissed her again and again before they took her away from me. Even in death she was beautiful. I felt she was free at last from all the demons she had faced and which had finally killed her. My angel girl had left this cruel life for a safer place. Goodnight my sweet child, you I couldn't have loved you more. I've no idea how to start to go on without you, I'm without words.

Someone took the initiative to call Darcy's dad, whilst I was in total unbelievable shock. He was informed about what had happened to Molly and he was asked if would tell Darcy, before she came home. I was so thankful that Darcy had been spared the pain of witnessing the events which had happened. It would have been unimaginable to even think Darcy might have walked into the house and witnessed what had befallen her sister, Molly. My mind continues to flash this horrifying picture every day of my life. How do I go on? Every day I struggle, every day I try to move on, it's too much for me to bear.

I now had so many unanswered questions, I began to write them down, and questions like:

I was confused about why the Mental Health team hadn't visited Molly, after she was discharged.

Plus other strange anomalies which, I needed answers too. I felt I'd dies myself, yet my brain was screaming out. I had to get to the truth, no matter how long it took me, I'd lost a precious daughter and there had to be answers as to why?

My heart was broken in two. I rang the doctor's surgery and was interrogated by the receptionist as to why I needed to see a doctor?

I wanted an emergency appointment I really did not want to discuss the terrors I had suffered with someone who I had no connection with. I did not want to talk about my daughter having killed herself over a phone with this unkind, uncaring human being. Even when I said, *my daughter hung herself,* it felt as if I'd just told her I'd had a tooth out. There was no compassion shown, this person, in my opinion, should not be working as a receptionist, in a doctor's practice, especially when they have no tact or common sense in dealing with the public.

I barely existed over many days just going through the motions by remote control. I was not sleeping or eating. In a moment of clarity though a thought occurred to me so I decided to make a list of all the things the people in mental health care in Burnley were desperately in need of. It gave me a focus something I wanted to happen. I was unfit to start things off myself but friends kept asking me if they could do anything to help me. So I contacted four people

Lucy, Olivia, Chantelle and Rachel and others who immediately set to work on the project.

Unity College where Darcy, my younger daughter attends and where Molly had attended had begun to collect absolutely loads and loads of useful items for the Burnley General Hospital mental health war, with a great deal of input by Miss Hill. There had been so many items bought for the mental health ward. They included. - Toiletries, games, books, jigsaws and an assortment of activities books and colouring books. I was overcome with their kindness and I'm sure Molly would have felt so emotional to see what Unity School had done in her memory, I'm sure she was looking down with that beautiful smile to warm all hearts that day.

There were also many contributions from people in and around Burnley. All these pickups had been arranged by Olivia, Rachel, Chantelle and others helped and worked tirelessly day and night collecting these items which were being donated. People gave generously So many people, good people, giving a tremendous amount of items like shoes, jumpers, coats dressing gowns slippers, socks, nightwear, day clothes, the list goes on and on. We had a full van full as well as five cars all stack high with all the things ready to take to the Burnley General Hospital Mental Health ward which brought the nurses to tears they were so overwhelmed by what had been done. I think we were all emotional as we stood there looking at so many boxes which filled a large room at the unit.

We had to wait before we were allowed to have a funeral for Molly. Booking the crematorium the undertakers and all the necessary things had to be done. We asked for donations for MIND to help all the people who have no-one to care about them and who are left in these institutions for years.

There is definitely a lack of funding for a lot of necessary things needed and so my life has involved trying to raise funds. Many people need to seek help with mental health problems and to be honest these services all have to be funded one way or another so even if it only helps a few I feel I have tried by best in Molly's name to be a part of doing this with so much help from friends who went that extra mile to make this happen.

I will never get over losing Molly, every day brings another sack full of cards and the doorbell never stops ringing, the house is beginning to look like a flower shop. There have been so many people who touched Molly's life and their outpourings of grief.

WE SAY OUR GOODBYES TO MOLLY

The funeral was finally arranged and with all the family pulling together we hoped we had done enough to make it as special as we could. It had only been a matter of weeks since she turned twenty years old and today she is gone. We thought Molly would want to be dressed in one of her lovely birthday gifts, a fluffy pair of pyjamas bought for her by her friend Chantelle and along with her teddy bear Snowbell who was tucked snugly by her side she looked as beautiful in death as she had been in life.

Her brother, Adam and her boyfriend Kirsten wrote beautiful eulogies you could have heard a pin drop as they had been read out. Although I was in grief and feeling bereft at that moment in time, I'm certain everyone in that room had felt the emotion, the hundreds of mourners standing outside the Crematorium, as well as the many inside feeling moved by the words spoken and the sheer volume of people touched by an intensity of such sadness. All of them, I'm sure feeling at sea, in the same sea, of swollen tears and sorrow. You could almost touch the outpouring of emotions. All her many friends and colleagues had been there from schools and colleges where, she'd once attended. Neighbours too, wanting to be there to pay their last respects. It had been totally, overwhelming.

A large framed portrait picture of Molly had been placed on a stand close to where she lay in the pure white coffin. It was so hard for me to accept she was no longer with us, in life.

Five hundred people, at a guess, came to Molly's funeral it was heartfelt and appreciated by all of our family. As the hearse moved slowly up towards the crematorium we felt so blessed to have the support of all these lovely people, who had known Molly in life, and those who hadn't, yet had felt the need to be there to give their support and had attended the cremation to give our precious Molly a great send off.

People travelled from all parts of Burnley and surrounding area. A great many knew her simply by being served meat by her at Andrew's Meat Stall, in the Market Hall, where Molly had worked for many years, starting as a Saturday girl, and had loved working there and chatting with the customers. It's those people who remembered Molly's lovely smile and cheerful nature, which always made them happy. Most of them expressed their feelings to me, saying how much she would be missed. So many heartfelt words and sad expressions, from Burnley people who had met her and had found it difficult, even to say her name an emotional outburst of never being able to see her again, with her having left this world forever.

I was choked, unable to speak, I was in too much pain and totally distraught to be honest, which you would expect. No child should die before their mother I would truly have given my life if I could have saved hers.

Even the music had been selected carefully, Kristen chose Ed Sheran *Photograph.* Myself I chose the other two pieces of music close to Molly's heart and shared memories. Lily Allen's *Somewhere* and the final choice had to be Eva Cassidy *Somewhere Over the Rainbow.*

Since then there have been so many questions keep going through my mind. Why on earth did Molly die? That's the question which haunts me. My parents and her brother and sister cannot accept the fact of what happened and as soon as I get stronger, a lady I know who is in a position to ask questions has already set things in motion.

After a recent meeting we have now been told a full investigation will take place and they will leave no stone unturned until they find out the facts which lead to Molly's death. It will take time, but I have all the time in the world, though nothing will bring her back. The meaning behind the songs meant so much to us all. The Lilly Allen song *Somewhere* was chosen by me because it reminded me so much of the special times when Molly and I walked to many beauty spots in and around Burnley. One of the special places was over the tops of Burnley at a place called Clowbridge Reservoir.

Since the funeral a group of her family and her sweetheart Kristen went along there and we let lanterns float above the reservoir in her memory. Sadly the weather was atrocious it rained heavily and we were soaked. I'm sure Molly would be not only smiling her lovely smile down at us but possibly laughing at us all. That was the way she always was in life.

The second music choice was chosen by me also *'Somewhere over the Rainbow'* the Eva Cassidy edition. I've seen so many rainbows of late and feel close to Molly every time one lights the sky.

Kristen chose the Ed Sheran song *'Photograph'* For them this had been their memorable song and one that make me sad if I hear it. Molly had known I wasn't a true fan of Ed Sheran and so it does seem pretty weird that every time I switch on the radio or go out to a café or restaurant his voice seems to haunt me. Or I tend to think it may be Molly's being a little mischievous to be honest.

I still feel a great deal of anger inside me that I should not have to grieve for my daughter. It seems to me Molly was unbelievably let down by the system. Life goes on, it has to and I'm trying to face the fact that Molly is not with me and our family but my heart is broken into, I'm empty. The flash backs are unbearable. Time and time again I keep saying.

'I don't know how I will survive, losing Molly, never to see her every again. I am, beyond words, I feel bereft, numb. The pain is indescribable?

The thing is I have to face the future without her, I really do. I have two other daughters and my son in my life, hey, I still have to work through this tragedy of Molly leaving us. Especially, for Darcy, she is still only a thirteen-year-old child. who is finding it very difficult at the moment? How on earth she'd even begin to make any sense of it all? She's a lovely girl, none of us can understand it. It's hard for her to understand why it happened. Like me, we break down in tears when her music is played and hug each other to comfort one-another. It's not easy to find a counsellor to help her come to terms and to get through her loss. Every day Darcy becomes more touchy and argumentative. I expect it's all part of the anger we all are feeling a feeling which, will lessen, hopefully, given time.

Anyone who hasn't lost a loved one, especially a younger child cannot appreciate the death of a young or for that matter older person. It completely devastates your life.

The pain is excruciating, it's absolutely hell, it never ceases. The feeling of total despair is overwhelming. Why, my Molly? Of all people, Molly would never have hurt anyone.

DOING MY BEST

I have had to resort to taking sleeping tablets. Once again, as the deprivation of sleep was affecting me on a daily basis. I knew I needed to have counselling yet have been told it could take over twelve months which was way too long a time to wait. Thankfully a friend of mine has found me some help at the Women's Centre in town and I have a meeting with her next week.

I saw a lady at the same bus stop as I always do in a morning, she always smiles though we've never had a great conversation but yesterday was different. This had been the morning that sort of changed. She looked at me and said.

'You look as if you're death walking.' She said.

I looked at her and I thought. Yes, I feel like death walking. I pondered a moment. She knew of course about the loss of my daughter but otherwise we hadn't conversed much. They say you sometime have this enlightening moment when things seem to click in your mind. For me this must have been one.

I arrived as normal at my morning job and was still feeling crushed but yet I knew for certain this was going to be the day that something changed. It was getting harder and harder to get up in a morning to go and clean at the large house. A house I had cleaned and looked after for more than eleven years. I had experienced a certain amount of bullying from the elderly nanny who looked after the kids and had done for a number of years. Although she was much older than me I'd always ignored her nasty vibes and snide remarks. Somehow this morning I just snapped inside me when she began her usual harassment.

She had no decency or compassion for me whatsoever. For God's sake my daughter had hanged herself and here I was taking all this crap off her, day in day out. I had no strength left in me to put up a fight. Instead I laid down my tools and walked away and to be honest I felt invigorated as I made my way back home vowing never to return. This was the turning point I needed.

Changes needed to be made and even if we have to go back to eating corned beef hash for a few months, so be it. For one thing I needed to spend time to grieve in peace and I totally admit I was, to put it mildly, not in a good place at that time.

The trouble is I'd felt I needed to look at my life and not waste any more of it on harsh and unthinking individuals who choose to make my life a misery. I cannot ever criticize my boss who was a lovely lady to work for and I've never had a wrong word with her in all the time I worked there. In fact, she was absolutely a hundred per cent understanding of me having to miss work during the time I had to help my son who was locked up in a Thai jail. She kept my job open for me and at no stage has she ever been unkind, but I think it was time to move on. She had given me an amazing reference and did ask me to go back to work for her, but it was never going to happen as far as I was concerned but I have nothing but gratitude towards her and will remain friends always.

Awoke this morning feeling like a great massive weight had lifted off my mind and it was time to take hold and begin again. My love, my thoughts for Molly, will be with me till the day I die, but I have to make sure I spend as much time as possible with Darcy and between us try to move away from all this sadness.

So, the first thing on the agenda is to have my CV typed up-to-date and list all my previous jobs. My good friend Sally had kindly offered to get it sorted out for me as quickly as she can because my new life needs to start as soon as possible.

The lady at the bus stop told me she's a cleaner at a job agency in town. She then told me more about the vacancies there. A Children's Home would be looking to recruit another member of staff as an Assistant for young disabled children. She arranged to go with me to have a look around this home. I felt comfortable the minute I walked through the door. The staff there are amazing people and put me at my ease straight away. I came away feeling good. It's true what they say when one door closes another opens and that sometimes, I'd like to believe God works in a mysterious ways.

LIVING WITH ANGER

Meeting my new friend at the bus stop seems to be fated in a way. She encouraged me to try something new. This has given me a different insight and I would love to work with these children I feel it would be a challenge but at the same time it could help to heal.

I'm not being pessimistic because I truly would like to work with these children but if I don't get a job working there I still feel changes are ahead for me.

I'm always assessing in my mind how Darcy is doing and for the moment she does seem to be her usual self yet time will tell. However, Katie my oldest girl rang me to say some girl on the estate keeps saying some awful things to her and it upsets her a lot. The girl in question shouts at her -

'So your sister died, get over it!'

I couldn't let go of one particular thing nagging away at me and that was the despicable woman who made Molly's life a misery at the workplace Molly had been assigned to. I sat there one night and scanned back through my phone messages from Molly and came across an incriminating account of what this woman had written by text message to Molly and the extent to which this woman had been bullying Molly and a full account of what that woman's constant bullying every day towards my daughter, whilst working there. It was all itemized in text messages sent from Molly to me on my own mobile phone. I took a screen shot of words written by Molly, who mentioned the bullying and I had forwarded them to the young man, who she had worked with, at the same office. I'd asked him to please show these text messages to the boss. I want him to know exactly what was going on at his office, every time he left the building. I wanted him to be in full facts as to what had happened to Molly, every day she had worked for him. She was only days away from finishing her work experience and would have left and away from that toxic person.

He believed everything I'd sent and agreed wholeheartedly with the emails. However, the boss was away on holiday so instead he must have shared them with the woman prior to the boss returning. She had simply walked out of the office that day and had not returned. There was no way for her to explain, guilty verdict as far as I was concerned. What a coward she really was.

Not letting go of this I found out where she was working and made up my mind to walk into the open office and confront her. It took guts to do this but I needed to get it all off my mind. In my mind, I had felt I had to do something; this woman was not going to get away with bullying my now deceased, child.

I went and sat in the coffee shop in town first and ordered a skinny latte and got myself into the right frame of mind. I then marched up towards the offices. Pushed open the door and made a bee-line towards her desk.

"Can I help you?" she says.

Looking up into her eyes, her face turned puce when she realized who it was.

'Take a good look,' I said. *'yes! I screamed. it's Karen!'*

She froze

"Yes! I'm Molly's mum!" I said. I'd pushed my face right up to her personal space.

'Molly the girl you tormented you bitch! You're disgusting, I hope to God nobody treats your kid the way you treated Molly!'

She didn't know where to look She began to squirm in her seat. By now all eyes had been on us.

"HER!" I said. The blood was rushing though my veins. I image it could be described a 'red mist' coming down or a moment of madness. All the pent up emotions made me snap I was doing this for Molly in my own mind. My eyes were watering thinking about my gentle sweet loving girl, who would be the first person to stop me had she been by my side. She would think people of **her** type are not worth the time of day.

'This woman,' I screamed, pointing at her face *'She's a nasty bullying moron! She loves terrifying young, defenseless girls, making their lives a misery with her vile poisonous tongue.'*

By now a member of staff comes walking over with anger in her eyes.

'Piss off.' She tells me.

Well that's appears about the level of the type of people she works with. *Lovely people who appear to employ; people like her, there*? I thought. That bitch is in good company.

I leave with my head held high.

I know I overstepped the mark, to be honest, but I felt vilified as I left the premises. Nobody should get away with the treatment she handed out to Molly, I felt I had fulfilled my responsibility as a mother and in future, I hope that woman will think twice before she treats another person in the same way.

Of course, I had been reported; I had a visit from a policewoman later on that evening.

Once I explained the circumstances and showed the officer the evidence on my mobile phone she immediately understood my anguish. I did give an undertaking that I would not be returning. This woman has a daughter of her own and maybe my words might have been taken on board and maybe she won't be as ready to undermine other younger kids who work with her. She would not like to hear her own daughter working in an office with a boss as vindictive as herself.

My emotions are all over the place, one minute I'm laughing the next I'm crying. I've been reading a few books on dealing with bereavement and how to cope and get through it. Apparently, it's normal for all these feelings to be expressed without rhyme or reason. I have to take things a day at a time that's what I'm now trying to do.

TRYING TO LIVE WITHOUT MOLLY

After almost beating the smoking habit I've sadly taken it up again, but again I had to have something to stop me from losing my mind. Since giving myself a talking to I intend to pack them in as soon as I can with the help of an ear gadget which helps to stop me wanting to smoke.

Apart from job hunting I've begun to take up my other hobby. The saw is out again along with my sander and electric screwdriver. The latest thing for me to do is to make beautiful glass bottles into lamps with fairy lights inside. They look pretty amazing and I intent to take them to a craft fair. There is still going to be good days and bad days but I will gain the strength to move on and this I intend to do but it's going to take a bit of time.

Adam took me and Darcy out to meet up with Kristen. He was telling us he'd managed to buy a small car. I couldn't help but think how proud Molly would have felt. I think it's good to keep in touch with Kristen who has lost so much too. He probably awakes each morning with one thing on his mind as we all do. Molly. The girl he loved so much and the girl who will never be able share his life with. They made such a lovely couple.

The latest news on funding for MIND is a sponsored walk. Many friends are organizing and advertising this event in the name of Molly it's so good to know her life wasn't lost in vain.

The Spiritual Church is having a medium in attendance during November to raise money for the same cause. Already it's a sell out and it's still a month away. Plus we have sold over £200 of raffle tickets and many prizes have been donated.

Something good comes from bad and with all the support for this cause is overwhelming. Molly would be so happy to see what money has been collected so far. There is a great shortage of beds, they need more staff, more facilities, and although the government is promising more funding there is an ever-present need which we hope to help fill.

Whilst Molly was in the mental health unit in Burnley there was a young woman in there at the same time who had three children. She sadly died whilst being in the hospital. It's terrible to hear such awful news. If money and help is not available to people when they need it I feel more and more, unnecessary deaths, will be recorded. There has got to be something done to avoid this. Sometimes people only need a matter of a few months intensive care and yet they are being discharged well before they should be due to the lack of beds.

The inquest on Molly's case is set to go ahead in February. I am being kept informed every three weeks to the progress and I want there to be a full enquiry about how unnecessary it was for Molly to have to die because of lack of qualified people making correct assessments. I feel she would still be with us if proper care had been in places.

In the meantime, I am still doing voluntary work at the Pendleside Hospice shop. Still enjoy the banter with the customers and my friends who work there. One thing I'm pretty good at now is working in sales. It's been said I could sell ice creams to Eskimos.

SOUL SEARCHING

This tragedy in my life not to mention my close family life was in turmoil. For me, life didn't go on I was barely existing. I felt desolate and out of control. My entire life had been turned upside-down, my emotions spiraled from being depressed one minute then giddy the next. I knew I was out of control, laughing hysterically one minute, then falling apart into a pit of doom the next. I even had felt suicidal and not wanting to live anymore. Yet how could I even contemplate death when I still have my youngest daughter and my oldest two, who are also suffering? My dear mum, who had never really recovered from the brain tumour she'd suffered from. I simply could not have to any either. I really couldn't.

"If only I had gone in your house half an hour ago, I could have saved her" Dad says. He had felt totally guilty that he could have saved her life had he gone back to check on her.

"If only I hadn't gone out that day, I sobbed… IF, IF.' I kept on and on.

Eventually we had to face up to the fact that we couldn't have known and none of us should live with that thought or we would have gone completely crazy.

It was up to me to stop this game blaming and I had to take control.

IF, as we all know is a little word, but turns on its head when faced with the absolute shock and despair we all felt. Hindsight is a wonderful thing, and we all have to remember that she had, for whatever reason, decided to take her own life, we have to live with the fact, we will never know what had gone through her mind that day, and we will have to live and having to accept we will never really know why?

It was not their fault nobody knows what was going through Molly's mind, not myself, or for that matter nobody could have dreamed what was to come, it's an unknown. Maybe it was on an impulse, a sudden feeling, or a moment of panic. I know for sure she would never have done this knowing that her young sister Darcy may have walked in the door and been the one to find her. That is something I'm totally sure of.

Of course we knew Molly was struggling with mental health problems. The fact, that a new medicine the hospital had been prescribed to her, and which, they were had been monitoring regarding the side effects, we were also aware of.

Molly told me she the only thing which helped make her feel slightly better was lying down and resting. Had I thought for one minute she had suicide on her mind, I would've had her with me every minute of the day. She had always told the psychiatrist and me, that she had never had suicidal thoughts.

We all have to find a way of coping without Molly in our lives and it will be hard and take a long while, she will stay in our hearts forever.

One thing I'm relieved about and that is Darcy didn't arrive home early that day or she would have seen her sister first it was me who faced finding Molly, it haunts me every day.

COUNSELLING

I knew I needed to see a counsellor, to help me cope. When I applied I was told there was a six months waiting list. I was advised to go and see someone at the Women's Centre in town who may be able to help me.

On my first visit at the Women's Centre I was not at all impressed as it began to make no sense to me at all. The lady who I was supposedly, getting help from constantly kept checking her watch. She made me feel I was wasting her time being there. I was made to feel my problems were of no interest to her and left. It certainly left me in no doubt that I would not be given the help I needed by this lady. That's the problem today when someone needs positive help from the mental health team there is never enough counsellors to give me or any other person the help they need immediately, not in six months' time.

After receiving a letter from the Investigator who was my only link to me getting to the answers as to what happened to Molly during her 13 weeks in mental institutions. I felt there was a lot of the questions I needed answers to which had not been listed on the letter of investigation. The questions only covered time spent in the various institutions with no mention whatsoever to the more serious and worrying nature of how Molly could possibly ended up killing her life.

I am not usually a vindictive person but someone obviously let not only me and my family down, but my daughter who pleaded for help and was left to do what she did.

Although she was giving me a lot of moral support at this time I needed to explain I was not happy with the questionnaire. I decided to ring her to explain my concerns. After a while she did return my call and we discussed the things which were worrying me and what I felt was not being addressed. She listened carefully then informed me she would seek an adjournment immediately effect regard to Molly's investigation which was due to be heard in February 2018.

She also said she would look into getting some counselling for me, which may take a little time but assured me she would sort it out in due course.

The questions which to my MIND and the ones I feel so utterly upset about are first of all.

(1) *Why did the health team not inform the family the new medication could cause 'low mood?' Also and more importantly I should have been made aware that sometimes this medicine causes young people to have suicidal thoughts.*

(2) *Why after monitoring Molly's heart rate and being told it was high and 145 and yet did nothing about that. She suffered chest pains and was rushed into hospital to be told they could not find her notes. (Why?) Also they put it down to a panic attack where I believe it had something to do with the medication which may have caused her heart to beat more rapidly. This scared Molly.*

(3) *Why when Molly pleaded with Patrick (her social worker) for him to do something for her as she felt unwell. She wanted him to get her some help immediately all he*

offered was to come back two days later to see how she was. One day later Molly hanged herself!

I very rarely get more than a couple of hours sleep each night and until I find a reason for why my daughter left us at the young age of 20 years old, I will fight on regardless. I don't want this to be a witch hunt but I do want to know what could or should have been done to save Molly's life. I cannot say a bad word about the nursing staff at Burnley General Hospital and the mental health staff they gave Molly proper loving care. With regards to the medical staff in all hospitals she went too I felt they didn't really give my daughter the care she should have received and for that matter didn't want to help me either I shall continue with my battle to get answers and in Molly's name I will leave no stone unturned to get answers as to why she died in vein.

I do have a few extraordinarily special people who are helping me through day by day in mind and spirit. Some are busy organizing more and more charity events in Molly's name for MIND.

There's had been a sponsored eleven-mile walk, and then later on. In November, it's the Spiritual Church event where we have 'An Evening of Clairvoyance' with Michael Magnem a well-respected spiritualist.

My battle with smoking continues and my appetite has gone even my love of walking has gone. I battle to get out of bed some days but have to go out and earn money. This I do by remote control, going through the motions not really being aware, yet still leaving houses clean and sparkling.

The fact people are contacting me on a regular basis, day in day out, and encouraging me to be part of the M.I.N.D objectives certainly keeps my mind occupied for a certain length of time. Already I have sold almost £50 worth of raffle tickets.

There have been people there for me even during the early hours of the morning at the end of a text message always ready to talk to me to stop me from dipping low. One of the main organizers is a dear friend Steve who I can't thank enough he's been my rock as well as Carrie, Sarah and her family. Joyce who sounds like my mother at times but she's been there for me. I'm so lucky to have this tower of support including Janet, Wendy, Gwyneth, Jayne and not forgetting Antony. So many people ringing me, my phone is never silent.

I recently read through the sympathy cards because I'd found I couldn't face it any earlier in all there was over 500 cards. Old people, young people, customers who knew Molly from serving them at Andrew's Butcher's in the market hall. One customer wrote saying Molly talked so much to them she had to recount the sausages she was selling them. She was so well loved by people. All those people, who I've never met before, but who had known Molly and had wanted to share with me how they'd cared about Molly. They wanted to share the times they'd had loved her banter. They gave up their time to show their respect for my daughter. All of these reminiscences helped me to smile again thinking how much my child had affected people's life in a good way. Without a doubt my little diamond in heaven has gained her angel wings staying forever young.

LOSING MY FAITH

Losing faith has suffered greatly I have not entered my church for many weeks. I'm hoping that given time, I will return at some point, but my faith has been tested to the limit and for now I still ask the question

'Where were you God, when I needed you the most?'

That may sound a little presumptuous of me but there's been too many awful times in my life and I thought I had begun to believe better things were to come and I was moving forward and changing the bad things into good things trying to move forward by choosing the right path and trying to do good things in life.

I'm struggling a lot with anger and resentment and because I am still living in close proximity to those *'girls'* I'm hearing from different sources the things they are putting out. Those same girls who, without a doubt, made Molly's life a misery makes my blood boil. Some days I could literally go and do to them what they did to Molly. It makes me want to scream when I hear that whilst we were at the Crematorium saying out last goodbyes to Molly they had gone abroad on holiday. I don't begrudge anyone a holiday and if they had only sent a sympathy card or even an expression of sorrow I could have, in time, learned to leave my anger behind. The fact that one of these bullies sent a text from their holiday destination asking:

"How did the funeral go?"'

How could they be so callous? To them it might have been some kind of a party they were asking about. I am disgusted to say the least. Most of these girls had been

Molly's friend since junior school. I can't express how young normal kids turn from lovely sweet girls into a bunch of bullies. And to be honest they are not worthy of the paper this is written on.

It seems someone who obviously feels as strongly as I do saw them out enjoying themselves down town in Burnley and decided to give them a taste of their own medicine. The only reason I know this is because I had a visit from the police to ask me if I was instrumental in this incident as they had gone down to the police station and told the police they had been threatened and I could have been behind it.

'I hope to God you're not going to come round here, every time one or all of them get accosted in town.' I told her, feeling the anger surge.

"Well," the police officer told me. We have to follow up complaints and they have reported the matter to the police and said it had spoilt their night out and mentioned you'.

"I had nothing whatsoever to do with it; I never go down town at nights to clubs or pubs I'm always at home taking care of my youngest child, Darcy. I don't even know what places they frequent or for that matter anything what-so-ever about them." I explained.

I pointed at the portrait of Molly surrounded by flowers. I looked into the eyes of woman police officer and told her.

"They might have had a night out ruined; I've had my life ruined for the rest of my life!"

She glanced up at the picture of Molly, surrounded by cards and candles from true friends.

"Sorry for your loss, we do have to follow up these things up." she said, with real sympathy in her eyes.

I did mention to tell her before she left..

"I'm a great believer in KARMA. What goes around comes around."

I walked her to the door knowing even a copper has feelings, though she has to stay impartial, I felt she had probably come across this type of behaviour before. I was grateful to her at least for believing me.

I'd felt on the edge and needed to get away from all this sorrow and although people had been wonderfully kind to me and my family with many expressions of love for our loss I knew I would sink lower and lower. I decided to and get away for a while and take Darcy with me. She was struggling too with all the comings and goings and having lost her sister so it felt right to get her away from the sadness.

I managed to pick up a cheap holiday to Greece thinking the sunshine and beaches would take away some of our pain for a time. On arrival everything was so quiet apart from a few older couples sitting by the beach just perfect for what we needed.

I was not pleased when I realized we had been put next door to two of the noisiest of holiday makers on earth! They were two young lasses, who had come there for fun, sun and excitement, and to party all night long.

Darcy and I had no sleep at all. I decided to go to their room and confront them. It all turned rather nasty and I ended up having a row with them. They in their wisdom offered me a line of cocaine! Almost telling me to chill! It all got out of hand and not long after that the manager came rushing over and said he was calling the police. Fortunately our Representative arrived and was able to explain what the situation was and finally things were sorted out and our point of view was accepted.

We were then transferred to a different room as we could not have gone on putting up with no sleep at all, it was becoming a nightmare being there as it had been for us at home. I know it's not anyone's fault but we needed peace and quiet and obviously they were young and wanted to party all night. I still struggled to sleep in any case but at least it wasn't loud music keeping me awake.

For the rest of our time away in Greece we managed to do what we wanted to do by going for walks along the beach, having a boat trip which is always a lovely calming experience and swimming. The food was lovely too and I felt Darcy had missed out so much quality time with me. After all I'd had to be visiting Molly in many different hospitals where Darcy wasn't allowed to go and then all the sadness which followed I felt I needed to make it up to her after all she's only thirteen. She is such a loving daughter and sensible but it's been incredibly hard as both our lives had been turned upside-down.

On arrival home though the depression, which really never left me, set in once more

Since finishing the cleaning job at the big house I had freed myself from not having to go there ever again. I had felt relieved. Every weekday, Monday to Friday, I don't think I've ever really given it much thought up to this point but I had allowed that women to bullying me for years without me realising it, or retaliating but maybe something snapped inside me and when I think about it I feel so much happier now not having to se

I've made good progress on creating a CV in readiness for new employment. I've also acquired three excellent references even one from my old boss at the big house. We've not fallen out at all I just cannot stand working with her nanny and it had to happen sometime. The Charity Shop Manageress has also vouched for my honesty and good attitude towards the customers so and so armed with my CV now and the references I'm ready to move one.

My crafts are growing by the day, making lamps from Gin Bottles or putting Christmas lights inside bottles and Candle decorations. They grow by the day ready for a Craft Fair which I intend to take them to within the next month. Steve has been so helpful getting me up and running with this and I'm looking forward to seeing how it goes. All these things I make are lovely for Christmas gifts so hopefully they will fly off the table.

I've been recently considering how on earth I am going to get through Christmas this year and out of the blue I made up my mind to volunteer be there for the homeless. I have contacted the food bank and offered my services for Christmas Day and I'm happy to say they've welcomed me with open arms. I was a little uncertain about Darcy it's going to be hard telling her. She can be with her Granddad and Grandma or her dad for the rest of the day. We will of course, celebrate Christmas together at my home on Christmas morning with Katie, little Harry, who bless him says every time I see him. 'Molly's up there in the clouds. My eyes run when he says that. He loved his Aunty Molly. As soon as the celebrations are over I'll leave to help to make the soups and butter bread and help to dish it out. In fact anything they ask me to do.

When I spoke about it to Darcy she reacted immediately.

'I want to help too. Can I come too?'

What a truly brave and lovely girl Darcy is. I wrapped her in my arms and we stood there hugging each other each both of the same mind. How much Molly loved Christmas.

Darcy's dad bought her a tortoise which is helping her to keep focused and has also given her a pet to look after. The fact it's a tortoise who she has christened Tommy she loves him but very soon he will be entering hibernation but Tommy has his own top of the range hibernation house. Darcy will be good and ready to see him again once we get into Spring, next year.

Things begin to slowly turn a corner I can see a light at the end of the tunnel. I think I'm even considering going back to church.

Then I get an email shattering my hope for a new start. I was cleaning at a client's house when the email came through. It was a message from Darcy's school which is a fifteen-minute walk away. I dropped everything and with the help my good friend, Steve, who came immediately to collect me in his car we reached the school within ten minutes of me having received the message. The message from Darcy's school asked me to go straight into school as there had been an incident involving my daughter.

'Oh God! What now?'

I prayed all the way down there that Darcy would be okay. With my heart in my mouth I arrived at her school, along with a very good friend of mine, Steve is the type of person who is always there when I'm faced with emergencies which, I must admit are becoming more frequent as time goes by.

Making our way down the corridor we entered the room. I was informed that Darcy had received a message on her mobile phone from one of the girls' who she shared lessons with. The message read:

'Get over it! Your sister died!'

I felt angry and upset that this should be happening to Darcy. The teacher explained that this behaviour was unacceptable and the girl would be dealt with in an appropriate manner. In the meantime, steps had already been made to transfer Darcy to other classes away from the girl in question so she would not have to be in contact with this girl who had caused Darcy so much distress.

I was only a matter of weeks since Molly had committed suicide mostly due to having been bullied and now it appeared not only had Molly had to face bullying from her friends now Darcy was being targeted.

When will this awful nightmare end and my traumatized mind find peace?

Darcy was still upset and it was decided I would take her home with me straight away. Luckily it was a Friday so she would have the weekend at home and once things had been sorted at the school she would return to take up her new classes, which Darcy welcomed.

This was the very last thing I was expecting. I'd had such respect for this school and the fact that Darcy was doing well academically and had settled well it only upset me more to think she was being sent such an awful text message, as this.

What could I do to protect her? We only live in a small town and it had only been a matter of weeks since her sister died. I certainly didn't feel I wanted to uproot Darcy and move her to another school for the sake of one person who was making Darcy's life a misery. It hadn't been that long since the whole school and it's pupils very generously donated many items to the mental health ward in Burnley to make sure the unfortunate mental health patients would have some small comforts in their lives by donations of nightwear, soap, towels, day clothes and the basic necessities and for them to get up of a morning and feel someone cares about them, to show them they hadn't been forgotten. Many of these people no longer have friends or relations to care for them. The National Health Service budgets cannot stretch to pay for the basic things they need, so it was unbelievably kind of the school to do this for them.

My feelings about what had happened were unimaginable. This was disgraceful behaviour, the person who said it, possibly needed some guidance herself, about right from wrong. However, I was grateful when I was told that since Darcy was seen to be at risk they would give her a 'free pass' to go and see a student support person called John who would be available to help Darcy if anything else like this occurred. After speaking with John I felt happier to know that Darcy has somebody to go to if the need presents itself. John appears to be a very likeable person and someone Darcy would not be scared to approach.

Since then it has caused me to feel more protective towards my family. I've already lost my Molly and now I feel one of my other daughters' is being made to feel unhappy. I have started to suffer panic attacks it has to be related to what is beginning to happen to my family. I feel as if we are all falling apart in some way or other with nowhere to turn. My chest begins to tighten, my face flushes up and I can barely breathe. It's difficult to explain but I'm sure anyone who has suffered this way knows what I mean. Once it passes I then have the worst migraine headache. It's just too much to bear, to be honest. I can be anywhere, like the other day when I was in Tesco Supermarket, the lady at the cash point noticed my face was flushed, blood was rushing to my head. I'd felt my chest tighten, I could hardly breathe.. She had immediately come to my help and made me sit down until it had passed and then helped me to pack my shopping. Thank God for the kindness of some people I felt so grateful she certainly made me believe in human kindness that day.

I have since visited my doctor and he has given me some sedatives to help me sleep and also something to help with the panic attacks and it is helping me a lot.

Now Darcy has settled to her new regime at school she looks much better and seemed to be a little more relaxed, which is helping as well. She's only thirteen years old and this is a very important time in her life in respect of her school work. She has always done well and works hard, so I'm hoping she will get through this next couple of years and do well in her exams. It's a difficult age for any child any case, without all the trauma and upset she had faced with the loss of her sister who she loved very much and now having to cope with the same thing, which was part of the reason dear Molly, took her own life, without doubt.

Being bullied, what a dreadful thing this type of behaviour is. It has always existed to be honest, but now with all the technology, mobile phones and text messaging it just wreaks havoc with people's lives.

As I looked through my front window, many months after losing Molly, I looked at the 1980s caravan which had still been left in situ on the drive. I had got all emotional and upset. The reason it was still sat there is because it was something' I'd bought for the day Molly would return home to us. Once she'd been discharged. How my son and I got it from Martin Mere to our home had been an absolute nightmare yet at that time it had been hysterically funny. It took so many stops and starts along the way. Martin Mere is in the region of 40 miles away from Burnley. The owner had offered it at a very cheap price if someone came to collect it. My son owned a very small vehicle, not equipped to pull a caravan. The caravan in question also needed a lot TLC doing to it to bring it back to life. We'd arrived back home at around twelve midnight and trying to get it in situ on my driveway had been hilarious, we'd pushed shoved and had slipped as we heaved it up the slope. What a time of night, in the dark yet laughing at the audacity of it all. I'm sure the neighbours were wondering what the hell had been going on.

It had brought all those happy memories back into my mind the day Adam and I had dragged this old wreck back home. It had also brought back the sad memories too. I hadn't know whether to laugh or cry.

As I had recalled the reason why I'd gone to such lengths to buy it in the first place. I'd thought it would be a wonderful thing to help Molly through her illness. I'd known she would need a lot of time to recover and in my way I was thinking ahead. Molly had been a talented and artistic person I'd known she would love a project of this kind, doing up the upholstery and making curtains and home-made cushions. I'd felt sure, together we would have put a sparkle of life back into this old un-cared for mobile home. It would be hard for me to let go of it.

I'm so happy I no longer waken up and have to go to my old cleaning job even though money is tight and I still struggle to pay the rent I'm determined to go forward and I will get other jobs to make up for the losses.

The investigation is still ongoing into Molly's death and I'm being updated every two or three weeks as to how it's going. The inquest is to be held in February but in the meantime the medical notes and a report should be made available for me and my family to go through with a fine tooth comb and for us to point out all the anomalies of what we felt went so wrong.

It's only weeks away from Christmas and even though I am not looking forward to it I have received an amount of money, which I had asked my previous employer, to put away into a Christmas fund for me. At least I have at some money buy my family a few small presents this year.

Darcy and I, as I mentioned a while ago, are to be volunteers at the centre for people who have nowhere to go or may be homeless this Christmas. At least they will have a good meal inside them and a few presents for the children.

We had already raised two thousand pounds for MIND by having a Spiritual night at the church in November. The medium was a gentleman who we have had before and he's usually quite accurate in his account of passing on spiritual messages to loved ones. We had so many raffle prizes donated and the Church was overflowing with people. What a night, all my family, apart from mum and dad who didn't feel they wanted to go and sadly Kristen, Molly's boyfriend couldn't face the meeting.

I helped by sorting the raffle prizes and setting them out at the front. Most of my family and friends were seated on the front row of the church.

The medium went from one person to another giving his readings. The spirits would come through to him. Then he turned his attention to my family. Molly was clearly getting her messages through to us all. The very first thing he said was

'I'm getting the initials DC'

I gasped - of course it was Darcy my daughter's initials. Tears started to fall as Darcy realized the message from Molly was aimed at her. She was all red faced, as she hates being the centre of attention.

The Medium continued. 'She is telling me'

"You can keep the three tops you've got your eye on."

Thankfully, Molly's message made the whole thing better. Darcy had loved three of Molly's lovely tops and so was stunned that she should mention them.

One minute we were laughing at some of the things she imparted which were totally true. Adam, my son was a butt of many of Molly's jokes, and he was taken aback to hear her speak so directly to him and said only things himself and Molly could have known about.

I know there are always non-believers out there but the Medium ended by saying – 'Molly is totally at peace.' At this point I spoke out. In my heart I knew she was at peace and we knew how much she was loved by all of us. We will miss her so much but for her to come through and make us all laugh again, what a tonic that was? Yet that was Molly, always a smile on her face and always had a great sense of humour.

To keep myself busy and my mind occupied as the days were lessening as Christmas approached I began to make special baubles in clear plastic with photographs of Molly with different friends as a special Christmas present for them to keep. I felt sure they would all love these baubles and would keep them as a token and a lovely reminder of their friend by putting them on the Christmas tree.

Ever since then I've been getting requests from other people asking if I can do the same for their loved ones after seeing the ones I have made. I've so many ideas going on in my head it takes it off thinking about Molly all the time and getting upset. Maybe next year I've been thinking I might try to do an on-line business selling some of my gift ideas. As I feel right now it's just not the right time to look into it but it's a possibility and another way for me to earn money to keep the wolf away from the door.

I've read so many different books now on mental health and getting how to get through bereavement and it has devastated me to read that one in four adults and one in ten children experience mental illness and that there are one million referrals to the NHS for talking through problems therapy. It's something which I whole heartedly believe is a very much overstretched mental health workers. More money and more nurses, doctors and carers need to be funded and much more should be done and this is something I am trying to do with a passion in a small way by raising as much money as I can.

MAKING AN APPOINTMENT TO SEE MY M P

Leading on from all this I felt I wanted my voice to be heard and I wanted to bring attention to the pain and suffering of so many people, not only me but everyone who's lives are affected and who's husband's wives and children are dying through lack of resources for mental health patients.

I made an appointment to see our MP Julie Cooper. Firstly, I needed to bring to her attention what had happened to my daughter and make people aware of how this could happen in this day and age. It could happen to their family next as it is happening to more and more people. I also asked Julie if she would come to the inquest on Molly which is to be held in February 2018, so she can see and hear for herself what happened to my twenty year old Molly. She has accepted my offer and is intending to get involved as much as she can to bring these issues to the public notice in any way she can and perhaps get help for her constituents in the Burnley and Pendle area. There are big changes to be made and if I have to go to the top to bring these matters to light I will do. I feel I have to for Molly. No-one else should have to die this way.

However, trouble looms its ugly head for Darcy again as two more incidents happen a few weeks later.

The first of the two was a boy who said to her she was fat and why didn't she kill herself! After he was interviewed he admitted saying this to her but was unaware of the fact her sister had died, although he apologized to her it was another hurdle for Darcy to face.

The second incident was, as far as Darcy is concerned was more terrible. She received another text from a pupil at the school. This message read:

'How did your sister die?"

Darcy replied to this message saying

'I don't want to talk about it.

I seriously still cannot comprehend the final reply Darcy received.

What did you do, stab her to death?

The girl in question was immediately excluded from school until they have had time to arrange a meeting with the parents.

I was exhausted, felt at a loss as to what I could do for Darcy at the moment, her life has taken on such a terrible amount of backlash since her sister had died. Isn't it enough that she's struggling to cope with that, without having all these other things happen to her? I know she's growing up and that in itself is hard enough, but seeing her so unhappy, day in and day out is unbearably hard as I can't seem to be able to reach her.

I wonder sometimes what kind of people would bully her in this way. Technology has a lot to answer for especially these days with everyone carrying mobile phones around with them it's too easy to do this cyber bullying. Bullying by media is without doubt done by utter cowards!

This type of thing should be acknowledged and spoken about at assembly in a morning to these sorts of issues, real discussions and stern warnings should be dished out to any teenager found to be sending threatening text messages. If they were older this type of thing would be classed as a criminal act, but of course, the majority of pupils are in the earlier teens. Especially the bullies!

Sadly I too suffered by allowing myself to be bullied this year. I went into this earlier in my story. I was so wrapped up in my grief it took me a while to realize what I'd been putting up with for months and one thing I will not tolerate is someone wanting to make me feel degraded and for me to be criticized for doing a hard day's work and taking pride in what I do. So, I fully understand how it's affecting Darcy she cannot walk out of school and forget about her education.

Changing school is not an option either this type of bullying is not something which is going to go away in a hurry. It's demoralizing and totally unacceptable and something needs to be done urgently in respect of Darcy. She only gets one shot at schooling and she's always been considered a conscientious and hard-working girl.

MUM HAS HAD A FALL

Life is just about plodding along so I decide to pay a visit to the Pendleside Hospice Shop where I had worked voluntarily up until the time Molly became ill and was moved from one hospital to another and then her sudden death. I met my friend Sarah again and it was good to start feeling a little bit like a normal person and not a zombie. My cleaning work up until this time had been hit and miss to be honest due to all that had happened and wanting to be with my family to help them too as much as I was able.

I was only just about got home and wondering about what to cook for tea when my dad came in from next door. His face was ashen and looked to be suffering from shock.

My heart almost stopped.

'Your mum's had an accident she's fallen and I've had to call an ambulance.'

"Oh, No!"

My strength was surely being tested again. I honestly didn't feel I could cope with much more.

Dad told me he'd rung at 2pm and it was 4.30pm before an ambulance from Stockport picked her up. Dad and I thought mum had broken her hip again, but until she was seen and examined we wouldn't know. After waiting for over seven hours at The Royal Blackburn Hospital, whilst mum had been given gas and air to relieve her pain, we were still no nearer knowing how bad her injuries had been.

I'd sat there feeling upset for mum but also it had made me think it hadn't been that long ago I was here visiting Molly at this hospital not so many weeks ago. The doctor finally came to see us and informed us that he wasn't happy with the x-rays so off we had to go again to the x-ray department to get more x-rays taken. Finally, the results of these showed no broken bones yet she wasn't able to support herself and walk at all. The corridors had been full of patients on stretchers waiting for attention. Mum at this stage had been lifted from the bed into a wheelchair, she'd been in agony and couldn't stand or move.

I felt it wasn't fair to blame the nurses for the long delays as they were all rushing around doing all they possibly could to see to everybody but the volume of people waiting for a bed was out of their hands. They can't be expected to find beds for people if there are none available. It was horrendous though.

Adam took me over the following night to see mum and nothing much had changed she still couldn't walk and was groggy with taking the morphine medication. It had been almost a week now with not much improvement. I felt really tired and depressed as we travelled back home, I could have slept for a week.

We'd had to leave and return back home, both Adam and I were exhausted as he drove the car home from the hospital. As he'd turned right onto our avenue my heart went into my mouth!

We could both see three police vehicles with all the lights flashing, all parked in a line outside my house and my dad's house with police swarming all over the road. I immediately thought something awful had happened to my dad, even thought my dad had died might be seriously ill or something bad had happened.

I could hardly breathe. Both Adam and I had jumped out of the car and made our way over to find out. My dad had only recently had a small stomach operation and was in recovery so I didn't honestly know what to think.

Although thankfully, the commotion was nothing to do with my dad at all, there had been something terrible going on two doors down from where I lived. It seemed unbelievable to hear that the neighbour, who'd we all knew well, a very quiet and kindly man, had gone to answer his own front door and was smashed over the head with a hammer. I mean, this sort of thing does not happen around here! We could not for the life of us understand why this seventy-two-year-old man should have been attacked in this way and what kind of unsavoury character could cold bloodedly attack him with a hammer!

From that night onwards the police had cordoned off the house no-one was allowed inside, not even his wife. I expect because the gentleman was still in a coma in hospital at Preston, it could well have become the murder scene. All we knew was he was in a very serious condition and may not survive. He had been taken to hospital in Preston where they had operated on him. What kind of person would do such a thing?

He is a lovely man with a family who has lived there for many years and is well known and well liked. A kind and friendly elderly man, who had done nothing at all, to deserve this tragedy happening.

After a police presence for more than a week in our area the police reported the culprit had been apprehended in Liverpool and had been charged with attempted murder. The victim still remains in hospital in a critical condition. We still do not know why this happened to him. All we think is that he had been targeted by mistake and whatever reason for this terrible act against a lovely neighbour is too upsetting for words. In fact, It could have been a close call as my dad was home that night and it could just as easily been him. It doesn't bear thinking about.

We all hope and pray for his wife's sake he makes a full recovery but he is an elderly man so it's hard to believe he will ever make a full recovery.

Many months later the man arrested was charged with attempted murder. He will not be eligible for an appeal for eight and half years. The motive is still no known, or at least had never been published. Sadly the lovely man and a neighbour of ours, who was badly injured, will never recover from the trauma of this and will spend the rest of his days in care.

On my next visit to the hospital to visit my mum, the nurses asked me if we could take her home in the car but it was simply impossible to lift her or try to get her into a car so they arranged finally to keep her in overnight once a bed was available. I finally returned home late and having to arrange to go back early the following morning, I felt like Florence Nightingale!

It was one day after another visiting mum and seeing so distressed. She was in agony and had been put on liquid morphine for the pain. Darcy went to the night visiting session but nothing had changed. After a week of being hospitalized they decided mum had to come home. She was really not well enough to be sent home with no back up from a district nurse as she could barely move and even with a walking frame she just leaned on it an dragged her legs. It was awful to see her like this and for dad in particular, as he didn't know how to help her. Getting her upstairs to bed took had taken us 30 minutes, lifting her carefully into a bed hadn't been easy either for dad, as he'd just had a stomach operation.

What a mess it all was, she shouldn't have been discharged home without some help arranged for her. The only diagnosis was that she had suffered damage to the muscle and it would take time to heal. To be honest, if I hadn't have been close on hand next door, it could have been much worse with both of them being elderly one or the other could have been injured lifting or falling and having an accident.

Apparently it's reported 374,000 NHS staff are off sick 25% of illness down to mental health issues and no wonder with the amount of stress and pressure they're under throughout the year. They are not super human and the GP's are often inundated with work pressures. There are occasions when staff are physically hurt or spat at by patients and it's so unfair. As winter looms I dread to think how much harder their jobs would get.

A sixty-day investigation into Molly's care and treatment was under scrutiny and I was anxious to hear exactly what had happened throughout this time to my daughter and to get answers to my many questions. I needed to know how things could have possibly ended the way it did. When it arrived there were 33,000 words in the medical report.

Apparently there are many failings but I'm told it's not about blame it's not about prosecution it's about making changes to the system. However, I do not intend to leave it at that so I decided to make an appointment with my MP to see if she could help me.

The following week I went to Blackburn to meet up with Julie Cooper and I was so wound up with pain and anger regarding the Mental Health situation I more or less gave out all my energy in getting Julie to listen and perhaps try to help me get some answers to my questions and also to help the many out there who are still suffering in mental institutions or being let down badly by the system and many young people are committing suicide. She was very understanding and when I asked her if she would come to the inquest on Molly in February 2018, which she agreed to attend.

I feel Adam still hasn't grieved properly yet and Molly's Grandma and Granddad suffer her loss on a daily basis, her grandparents, had been a bit part of Molly's life, she was never away from their home, even sat with them on a Saturday night to watch TV and have a good old laugh. She'd loved them so much.

Kristen has gone back into work, he too, is suffering. After all they were childhood sweethearts; I doubt his heart will mend for a long while they loved each other so much. His dad, Howard and his step mum Laura are constantly in touch with me and have been a tower of strength to us all. They feel as much as we do because of Kristen and I care so much for them all they help me so much when I need them. They brought me a beautiful Christmas bouquet.

Even my old boss turned up with a lovely plant arrangement. People have been so gracious to me and I've felt constantly overwhelmed by their constant care.

Molly's hospital notes have finally arrived and it took me over five hours to read through them. There is so much wrong with this report I have decided to seek a solicitors help in getting to the bottom of things. I will never be able to bring Molly back but I will do my total best to see she didn't die for nothing. Errors have been made and I am not seeking revenge or money only justice for my daughter who lost her life in vain.

I'm trying my best to make the most of Christmas even though being without Molly is constantly with me I decided to take up the offer from Carrie a friend of mine to go to an auction in-between Christmas and the New Year. Carrie constantly to try to cheer me up. She has a great sense of humour and really did help me at that time to laugh a little. So was Sarah. Being with them both makes me forget and it also does me so much good. Thankfully, I was blessed with a good sense of humour too which is what I feel gets me through each day.

My mother is gradually getting about a little better though she far from being able to walk unaided. For a little fun Darcy tied two bows on her Grandmas walking frame for Christmas. It's a laugh a minute when I go to their house and listen to them. One of them is slightly deaf and the other an invalid and on morphine. The mixed up conversations are hilarious. Oh life can be fun for a moment or two!

What a turn up this was. I was told the waiting list for counselling was twelve months. Amazing, when you think about it. Word must have got out about Julie Cooper getting involved and maybe there might be a little bad press coming up. Surprisingly I get a phone call the following day to say I can start counselling this coming Monday. Life is funny sometimes.

I feel it is time to sell the caravan because I know my heart will not be in it to turn it into a comfy homely space without Molly's input so I thought it was time to say goodbye.

All the amazing presents I received were special and although I wanted to get people something nice I only managed small items. I hope they know how much love I put into them though. I have to be careful with my money as bills and rent had to be paid first. It's hard being the breadwinner but I've succeeded in the past and hopefully 2018 will be a better year for us all.

Darcy still has her ups and downs as you would expect but seemed to have settled to her new regime at school she looks much better more relaxed, which is helping me as well. She's only thirteen years old and this is a very important time in her life in respect of her school work. She has always done well and works hard so I'm hoping she will get through this next couple of years and do well in her exams. It's a difficult age for any child in any case, without all the trauma and upset she has gone through with the loss of her sister who she loved very much. Now having to cope with the same thing which led to her sister Molly's death. Being bullied. What a dreadful thing this type of behaviour is. It has always existed to be honest but now with all the technology, mobile phones and text messaging wreaks havoc with people's lives.

Christmas Day arrives and the only good thing at the moment is that I've managed to kick the smoking habit again. I expect the shock of everything which had happened started me off but I honestly can't afford to smoke so it's a 'no brainer!'

On Christmas morning we opened our family gifts then Darcy and I went to see Harry my grandson who is five years old. He always asks if Molly's coming. We tell him Molly's in heaven but it's so sad, she adored him. We watched him open his presents *a glow in the dark race track,* which his uncle Adam bought him and he loved it, He then opened his other present from his uncle to find he now has a keyboard to play, which will more than likely not please his mum, Katie, to be honest.

It was then time for Darcy and me to go to Spiritual Church as volunteers for the day making food and wrapping presents and chatting to people. I just couldn't have faced being at home. Adam had decided to go for a curry with a friend and I felt my mum and dad just wanted a quiet peaceful day none of us felt like celebrating to be honest.

Whilst wrapping up parcels and sharing the sellotape with a lad called Will we chatted. It's strange to think why certain people come into your life. He told me his friend had committed suicide only weeks before Molly had so I obviously felt an affinity towards him in that sense. When he told me he'd set up a music event to raise funds for the Samaritans it inspired me. He had also set up a panel of care professionals to answer questions. I was very impressed by what he told me.

He had raised the same amount for the Samaritans as I had for MIND £2,000 so we had a great deal to talk about. I felt I had met someone with a big heart and someone I may well keep in touch with and hopefully we can join forces at a future date and organize a music festival or something similar to raise more money for both our good causes. we shared a few Christmas crackers and out of one of a cracker was a green frog, he managed to shoot it into the cup before me and to be honest what started off to be a day of dread ended in me feeling uplifted after speaking to someone who really lightened my day. What a good person he is and someone who, I felt, understood how I was feeling.

I left to go to a friend of mine house who was having a small Christmas buffet. She was there wrapping a very large parcel for me it was the size of a small boy. I found out later it was a rather large candle holder after it took me an hour to unwrap it. Carrie always makes lovely buffets and so there was plenty to eat.

Finally I arrived home tired and in a way relieved the day was almost at its end. I had received so many gifts some lovely pictures of Molly one in particular was in beautiful framed and lit up. I also received so many different types of candles, which I do truly love having around me. For now though I wanted a few moments of silence in my own space with just one special candle glowing. I close my eyes and know I am never alone Molly's is never that far away sealed in my heart.

I planned to have a quiet Boxing Day although Darcy and I will be going out for a meal with good friends for a curry. I will not celebrate by drinking too much alcohol but I know by bedtime I will be enjoying a nice Baileys Coffee Liqueur, which Adam bought for me.

NEW YEAR 2018

I could hear the fireworks exploding outside the house as I sat and dwelled on all the things I've faced throughout 2017. I had been invited to a New Year's party, but my heart hadn't been in Christmas or the New Year to be honest. All my family felt the same we have all suffered the most horrendous year of our lives.

I had been invited to a New Year's Eve party, but I certainly was not feeling the joy of New Year at all. I had made a nice meal for Darcy, my other daughter Katie and grandson Harry.

Well, it might be a new year but it's far from a happy one for our family this year, in more ways than one.

Dad came in from next door to tell me mum had fallen again, this had been one of the many times since having been previously discharged from hospital. Dad had been struggling to do what he could to do to help her and I would also nip next door to give dad assistance, especially when she had fallen, it was difficult to lift her up without help.

You might say it was an accident waiting to happen. The fact, it was possibly the worst time of year to be ringing for an ambulance. After waiting a very long time for the ambulance to arrive and then we had to wait a further six hours in casualty, to be seen by a doctor. My mum was screaming in pain and they needed to give her some gas and air to help curb her suffering. The corridors were full from end to end with people all needing attention.

I'm still undecided about what to do about the money raised. Most of the money up until now has been donated to MIND. Yet after speaking to Will during the Christmas period, who told me had sadly lost his best friend to suicide. I had considered including The Samaritans as another good cause. This still comes under the heading of mental health care. I feel whatever monies are collected though should go to our own local area in Lancashire.

I 'd still to speak again with Julie Cooper our MP to ask her advice as I am still awaiting the outcome of the investigation into Molly's death. I'm informed at the present time that no-one is to blame which makes me shudder with anger. I still feel someone should be made accountable for why Molly Had died. Mistakes were almost definitely made and it's not about being vindictive it's about getting to the truth, nobody should have had to suffer in the way

Molly had and I truly hope that this new report will at least bring me the answers to why? Why did my daughter die? More to the point that, in the future lessons may be learned even though it's too late for my daughter as nothing will ever bring her back, I do not want her to be forgotten and in her name for my own peace of mind I have to find out why she died in vain.

More information leaflets, more contact numbers etc., the system in the mental health is desperately in need of re-organization and recognition for those in the community who need to know where to go and who to see and get the best advice and better information available.

When I did finally receive Molly's hospital notes. I was not upset I was enraged by the contents, over a thousand sheets of paper! This was the moment I decided I needed to seek a solicitor's help. There in the notes a list of so many failings throughout her thirteen weeks in mental health care which I am not at all happy about.

I cannot go into details at this time for legal reasons but I intend to follow through with this once the inquest in February gives me the true facts in black and white as to how the system let my daughter down dreadfully.

My GP told me the waiting list for grief counselling has a waiting list of twelve months which, if you consider how badly I and probably so many people needed mental health treatment, is not at all helpful.

However, strange as it seems after contacting MP, Julie Cooper I have since been switched to a much better time period it's now been reduced to ten weeks at a minimum.

This is unbelievably good news for me but I did feel it sounded a little like it's not who you are but perhaps the fact someone like Julie Cooper could make a difference and I have a lot to thank her for. I'm only unhappy that my daughter, Darcy is considered too young to be considered for adult counselling but I am still doing my very best to try to get her the help she needs to get through such an horrific year and all the other things she has been targeted for. I'm just hoping Unity College, her present school, will strive to do something to help her, especially regarding the bullying she's has had to cope with.

TOTAL EXHAUSTION

So much had happened and my body was showing signs of exhaustion. My coping mechanism had stopped functioning, not surprisingly due to the strain of Molly dying and having to keep going despite the workload, funeral arrangements, people constantly visiting to commiserate and then the efforts being put into raising funds for MIND, it stands to reason this would happen at some point. I know that under normal circumstances, I'm a strong person but I'd not allowed myself time to grieve properly, or even come to terms with the tragedy of it all.

Before I knew it February had arrived and despite my own health problems, the Inquest into Molly death had to be faced. Arranged for the 14th of February 2018, of course, it was Valentine's Day. Another date, to log in my long lists of awful memories I'd felt numb, unable to deal with what the outcome of the court's decision. I'm not particularly knowledgeable, in respect of court procedure or the correct protocol, in a court situation. Yet, I had known deep inside, I did need support. Support from a qualified person in law, it was decided we would seek that advice from a Solicitor who could look at the medical records and would examine the paperwork to see what mistakes had been made during the 12 weeks Molly had been in the mental hospitals prior to her committing suicide. Something wasn't right, I was confused and totally out of my depth and in no state to fight or deal with this on my own.

Thankfully, the Solicitors have agreed to represent us at the Court Hearing, which, when I think about it now had been the greatest help we could have wished for.

On the day itself, Adam my son and I arrived at the hearing together with our Solicitor. Having to deal with an inquest made it more real. Everything was out in the open. Molly's life under scrutiny and examined by all the medical experts, NHS workers, with was being discussed. Our Solicitor had put forward legal paperwork into the court prior to the Hearing on our behalf. I wasn't feeling well enough to take in much of what was happening, to be honest. One witness, the Solicitor acting for the Bradford Clinic had stormed out of the hearing in a very unpleasant manner. There were people there who I would clearly not have wished to have seen, but apparently this type of thing is allowed, despite me, as Molly's mother, having justifiable reasons to object.

In the event, after waiting what seemed liked hours, the Inquest was adjourned and expected to take place in September of this year, to allow time for all facts and reports to be obtained, before the Inquest can be re-opened.

Still ongoing, at this time, was Darcy's immediate problems. It was obvious she was desperately in need of counselling. She was still having to cope with her sisters' death as well and the ongoing bullying. There is a great shortage of counsellors. This was apparent, during the time of Molly's illness, too few experienced nurses, caring for the mental health patients. Darcy had already waited six months for an appointment. For something as dreadful as this, it should have been a priority, her life was in a total mess and she is only thirteen years old, it's deplorable she wasn't able to get the help she needed urgently.

When spring arrived, I was in a sorry state, unable to move or motivate myself. My autobiography book had been left to idle on the computer. Getting out of bed in the morning had proved hard. I felt sluggish, went around in a fog most days. Prescription drugs for the constant panic attacks, sleeping pills to knock me out at night only rendered me inadequate to cope with everyday chores. Every day I'd open my eyes and see Molly's face. Ed Sheran music was constantly being played wherever I went, (he was Molly's favourite singer). Every time a rainbow appeared in the sky, it brought me to tears, another memory of Molly. The awfulness of finding Molly on that fateful afternoon fills me with horror and sadness at the same time, how does anyone even begin to deal with that?

My birthday followed and not many days later it was Mother's Day. All I could do had been to think of Molly. I picked up the cards she had sent me the year she'd died and wept. Molly had always spent a great deal of time choosing the right present. Always got the right words, the much-needed present, so much loving thought went into any present purchased for anyone.

Many of Molly's good friends had arrived with bouquets of flowers and cards with such loving words. There had also been the kindness of many good friends, remembering and posting loving messages on my Face book page. I'd felt overwhelmed by all the kindness, yet at the same time, found myself drowning slowly in grief. I was totally unwell, eating little and asking myself over and over again WHY? Why did Molly die? She had never intimated at any time to the family, or her physicians she wanted to kill herself.

To be honest if it hadn't been for my thirteen-year-old daughter, Darcy I may just have curled up and slept forever. I kept telling myself I will become strong. I will face another day without fear without dread and without Molly. I am a mother first and needed to be there for Darcy, we are all suffering in our own way. My mum and dad are devastated, Molly was their life, and she was treated like their daughter and loved so much by them. It upsets me on daily basis to see their hearts broken and to have to see how lost they are without Molly.

Sometimes I feel I have nothing more to give of myself, other than to make sure my parents know I'm only next door, they can call on me day or night if needed. Nothing I do makes me feel any better, the death of Molly has overshadowed every day of my life since the 26th August 2017, the day I held her in my arms, the sudden loss of my precious child. I still have to live though. I have to carry on the best way I can and try to keep the family together, hopefully coming out the other side with hope and a better future, never forgetting Molly, but having to learn to live without her.

Those in charge of my mental health state at this time, had deemed it necessary, to treat me as a priority case, but could only offer me some temporary counselling. A lady named Susan had been appointed to me and after two sessions with Susan, it had become clear she might need counselling herself? After spending time listening to me! At our first meeting I told her I was two different people, Karen number 1, was deemed to be, by my peers, a strong purposeful and helpful person with a great sense of humour.

Karen number 2 had the complete opposite persona. She turned into a monster when faced with any of Molly's tormentors. This Karen would totally lose the plot by approaching them aggressively. The anger in her, held no bounds, I related this person to *Susan*. Karen number 2, would, in a moment of madness or have a *'red mist'* moment, explode into expletives and indescribable anger against the people who, I she'd believed and still does believe, had helped to put Molly where she was to end up in, a psychiatric ward.

Needless to say I was reported to the police for my outbursts. Of course, they paid me a visit on a number of occasions, throughout this phase. Although, I avoided arrest, I did feel there was a God after all, when the police saw the picture of Molly on my wall and heard my explanation, they as human beings, accepted my grief, letting me off with a caution.

Finally, the day arrived for Darcy to go to see a counselor after a seven month wait. Her meetings were to take place at her school, in the beginning, since that time she now goes to a group on a Friday night, which to my great relief is helping her a lot.

There have still been incidents along the way, which I've had to deal with and make a stand about with her, but I feel progress has been made and together we are coming to terms a little with our grief and becoming friends as opposed to at times, enemies. It's a well-known fact, when you are hurting you take this anger out, (usually on your nearest and dearest), so being the mature person in this instance, I have weathered the storms with Darcy and I'd prayed to have the same closeness as I'd had with Molly, going forward.

I still have many uncertain feelings about life itself. I have good days and bad days. Sometimes, I can't even raise myself in a morning to have a shower or function in a normal way. I'm told this phase will become less and less and ease in time. On my worst days I avoid contact with everyone, feeling empty alone and dead inside.

A MEMORIAL DAY FOR MOLLY

The month of May brought better weather and a reported heat wave on the way. I'd been contacted by phone from Molly's College in Nelson, where Molly had done her hairdressing training. They had arranged for a Remembrance Day on 14 May 2018, and of course I was asked to attend and maybe give a speech, I declined to do a speech, but was happy to attend.

Molly's death had affected many of the young girls, who had been at college with Molly. It had been because of the nature of Molly tragically taking her life; the college had decided they needed to hold this Memorial Day. Not just for Molly's sake but for the mental health of the girls whose grief over Molly was still raw.

On Memorial Day a speech was given by someone whose life had been affected by mental health. She spoke openly to the audience, telling us of her depression, the bullying and the time she came close to killing herself. Everyone needs a friend, she told us, for her, she was only alive today, because she did have that special friend. She'd been pulled back from the brink. It was her friend who persuaded her to live and not to take her own life. She said she was one of the lucky ones to be here to tell her story.

Talks were given from NHS nurses, they spoke about mental health issues, video footage was displayed and speeches from people who had known Molly spoke so lovingly of the. Some people, who I'd never met before, but had known Molly from college, spoke to me about the Molly they had known, it touched my heart to hear their memories, though it was a tough day one way or another for me to deal with.

It had been made clear on the day that there's always help out there if young people experience bullying or feel depressed. They can approach a teacher, or find out about groups within the education system, which anyone can access, that they should never feel there's no hope.

Following on from this, we all went outside to the bench which was situated in the grounds. Balloon was tied to the bench with Molly's name on then they flapped wildly in the wind. Music by Coldplay played (not really the song I would have chosen), then a choir sang, bringing the service to an end. Many joined together to walk two miles, from the college to the Victoria park, to show their support. I sat there on the bench, feeling empty, this feeling rarely leaves me. There wasn't a dry eye at the memorial as we all reflected on sweet Molly.

Someone contacted me, once again from Nelson and Colne College, this time to ask me if I would I talk about my daughter's suicide on 2BR Radio which was going out live on Mental Health Awareness Day. Seems they had a few people who would be speaking about the loss of child or a family member, through mental illness.

I didn't feel I could go on air without breaking down, so two of Molly's good friends Chandelle and Kim, as well as Molly's dedicated teacher, Claire had summed up Molly's life in a touching way. They spoke of the many times they'd shared with her, what she'd done or said to make them laugh, it was so typically, Molly. She was always happy and did have a chatty nature. They all managed to get through the interview without breaking down, they made me feel so proud to have been Molly's mum.

The money raised by Nelson and Colne College on Memorial Day was collectively joined to since Molly's death, in total, amounted to well in excess of £l,000, These monies have now been shared between a local charities MIND, 'Action for Young People'. A similar amount to 'Young People with Issues'. Also a charity called Bright Lives for Children in the North West. They provide mental health groups for those who Self Harm, Anger management, and Bereavement Counselling.

This service is proving to be a great help for adolescents, especially Darcy, my younger daughter, who is receiving ongoing counselling and help since becoming out of control, due to bullying and, of course, bereavement issues. Thank God, she is improving on daily basis and thank you to all those people, who are doing a great job. The only downside is, the waiting times for these treatments, they must start to be treated more urgently and for counselling to be more speedily accessed.

OUT OF THE BLUE

Out of the blue I'd received a letter, I'd felt it had been sent to taunt and had unsettled me. The letter had been written by one of Molly's *so-called* friends, an ex- friend since the Parklife episode. He had mentioned in the letter that he'd written it on behalf of the other, so called group of friends, who had supposedly been Molly's friends. (In my mind, the very ones who'd let Molly down.). It went on to say he's sorry to have let Molly down, telling me how he prays for me, (the letter beggared belief!) He then tried to explain how much they all miss and loved Molly and how it has affected their lives.

They still **have** their lives. Molly is no longer here. Also, whilst Molly was extremely ill, over a thirteen-week period and hospitalized, not one of these **so called friends**, rang, or had sent a text message or sent one single note to affirm what this letter is trying to say.

The truth of the matter is that, as far as I could work out, they are self-absorbed, trying to absolve themselves, whilst attempting to save their own backs. As I understand it, I've been informed they can't go out anywhere in Burnley town centre. The venues, where they are known, and with having to deal with people making them feel uncomfortable.

They were without doubt, being victimized. I had no knowledge of anyone who had been verbal towards them, it could possibly, have been, half of the young people who lived in Burnley. Molly was so loved. My postbox over the last 16 months is full of support from many people I have never met, who feel anger about how Molly had been horribly treated by these sad individuals. On the day she should have been enjoying herself at The Parklife Yearly

Event, for charity. She had ended up later that night fighting for her sanity in Burnley General Hospital.

These friends, I understand, were abroad enjoying a nice holiday in the sun whilst Molly was being incarcerated. In my opinion, they need to pray for themselves, leaving messages on Facebook, quote : *Molly faking illness*? All I can say is, you have to live with those types of comments. Not one of you showed the love you profess to have had for my daughter. Real friends do not do that to people they love.

DATES I HAVE TO FACE

The next hurdle, I'd had to face this year had been to face the fact it would have been Molly's 21st birthday in July. To write this down had torn me apart. Who on earth buries their child before they are twenty-one years old? A few family and close friend of Molly's took twenty-one balloons up to her favourite place at Clough Fold Reservoir in Rossendale. This was what I'd preferred, a small gathering of the people, she dearly had loved.

I had this feeling Molly was looking down laughing at me, as I tried to curl the satin ribbon's, attached to the helium balloons, it had cut into my finger. (always things like this happen to me). That's the sense of humour, we had always shared, and Molly would always laugh at me in the face of adversity. Letting go of the balloons I silently whispered to myself, fly high my angel, miss you, love you'. Not wanting to turn my head away until the very last balloon had disappeared above the clouds and out of sight,

We'd had previously arranged to have a meal, across the road from the Reservoir, at the New Wagoner's Inn. None of us felt particularly hungry though, so we shared a large plate of chips, between us, somehow it didn't seem right to be celebrating to be honest.

That evening many people brought me presents, I felt so touched by how some people do understand, and not only that, they come personally to see me to show their feelings which was so very kind.

Molly is with me always in my mind, her favourite songs, the smell of her favourite perfume, even the smell of certain foods. I still feel the anger and resentment to those people who let me down, even I may add, some family members too, who sadly don't realize how hard it has been for me to let go, I take everything personally, it's more than likely the medication for anxiety attacks. I possibly blow things out of proportion,

Many months ago prior to losing Molly, I had written on more than one occasion to the hospital management about the unsatisfactory treatment Molly had been receiving, by certain members of staff, at the many establishments where she'd been sent. Weirdly, this had been a matter of eight months previous. It was only after Molly's death the hospitals deem it necessary to answer those letters of complaint.

I do have to say I'd received a lot of help from our town's Member of Parliament, Julie Cooper. Around that time, she'd helped in many ways and made herself available to me after Molly's death.

Five months had elapsed since I'd heard anything from the Solicitor. I phoned up to ask for an update as to how things were progressing and if a date had been set for the Inquest. Apparently, they were still waiting to receive documentation from one of the hospitals involved. I was no nearer knowing, as to when, the Inquest would be taking place.

So many questions kept running through my mind in respect of medical neglect. I was still waiting to hear and needing to know why Molly had been moved so many times from hospital to hospital and what had happened to her. I have to get closure to these harrowing events, for peace of mind. This will not happen until the inquest goes ahead and all lines of enquiry are investigated before I am able to move forward.

I will never give up until all relevant issues have been examined, but I do feel we have a strong case. I was with Molly relentlessly and I witnessed what treatment was given to her. On one visit to Bradford, I saw how tranquilized she was after being given a strong drug, which had reduced her to a paralyzed Zombie. I took a picture of her sitting on a bed unaware of anything at all, not even her turning to look at me and her family.

For Molly's sake we have to get to the bottom why she had been let down so badly and whether the powerful medication she'd been given had affected the state of her mind.

For weeks on end I had been constantly see-sawing backwards and forwards, over a period of six to seven weeks. I'd be lost inside myself for days, unable to get out of bed, or get dressed or motivate myself. Other days I'd be up before daylight acting like a superhero, covering a million tasks, cooking, cleaning like a maniac, gardening till dusk.

There were a few special people who kept in touch throughout this period on social media. These people were there ceaselessly, sending messages to me and talking to me with me until late into the night. They worked so hard, to encourage and console me and doing their best to cheer me up and trying to bring back laughter to my life. Then I'd wake up after less than a couple of hours sleep, the panic attacks would take me over. Palpitations would follow; my heart would beat so loud in my chest I was certain I was going to die.

Those people, they know who they are, and I want them to know, I could not have got through these never-ending days without there kindness. I shall never, ever forget what they did to get me through.

It's no wonder when I'd given it some thought, what my daughter Darcy must have been going through. She was slipping away from me, constantly misbehaving. I was being contacted by her school letting me know she had been leaving school without permission. She'd started getting into bad company, smoking, and staying out, having me in a constant state of worry.

I'd sorted out some counselling for her at church. Mandy, a lady at the Spiritual Church had helped Darcy as much as she could but it would take all of us many months or even years to deal with.

Finally, I slowly began to go out, encouraged by a friend of mine, who I made arrangement to meet with once a week at a coffee shop. It took my mind off my own worries and trouble to be honest. Sharma is a totally inspirational woman. I sat with her listening to her explaining that she suffers on a daily basis. She suffers from a long term illness, and needs to take 115 tablets a week to stay alive, but hell, it's was not taking away her ability to enjoy life and have a good laugh, Within minutes of ordering our coffees she had me in stitches, laughing They say laughter is good for the soul.

It felt good to get away from domesticity and my own troubles for a while, even though my stress levels were through the roof, I was slowly falling apart. Yet listening to Sharma talk had been a real tonic and was just what I needed.

My family life at this point was going downhill fast, all my children were falling apart, and we were all suffering in our own way. None of us were in a good place. We all needed some kind of help before we all went under. It broke my heart, seeing this great gaping hole appearing in our close-knit family, something I feared which, we may never quite recover from.

SPIRITUAL HEALING

Since pretty much abandoning my local Spiritual Church, I had heard there would be a Spiritualist speaking at the Colne Spiritual Church, about six miles out of Burnley. No-one would know me there, so I had gone along to see if she would single me out from the many people who attend these \spiritual evenings.

The minute she had stepped out onto the stage, she had a spiritual message which she directed at me, she simply said, *I'm giving you some red roses for love, and your Nana sends you a hug.* This helped me enormously, I could not have asked for more. Molly always bought me roses, and rainbows were always a sign between us.

Trouble knocked on the door again, Darcy had been involved in a serious misdemeanor at school, which I needed to go and speak to them about. This time it was totally unacceptable, so much so, it was something I would be unable to deal with on my own. I had spent many long discussions with her dad in order to get his support. What she had been involved in that week was out of order and out of character, strong discipline had to be put in place.

Between her dad and myself, we worked out a rota, whereby either he, myself or her granddad took Darcy to school got her signed in at school every morning, then arranged to have her collected at the end of the school day. Something serious had to be done to nip things in the bud before she would go completely out of control. She was grounded throughout the whole of the six week school holidays, no access to her mobile phone (this was confiscated by her father who had been financing it for her).

The school holiday had been a matter of a couple of weeks away at that time, but I had been adamant she would be watched and monitored and treated like a child, (which, of course, she still is), until she accepted that what she was doing, was wrong. She needed to know her behaviour would not be tolerated. Neither her dad nor I would sit there and allow her to behave as badly as she had, without her being made to learn respect.

It's been hard sticking to our agreement, but little by little time has passed and Darcy is turning a corner. I pray that our good relationship will carry on now. During this six-week period, we've had sulks, had a few arguments and attitude going on. Yet, we stuck to the new rules.

Getting it all out slowly and building a special trust together Darcy had helped me with planning and decorating her bedroom. I bought some new furnishings and assembled them and now it looks a lovely room, which she appears to love. Gradually, given time, it began to dawn on Darcy, we were not going to give in, or give her any freedom until we had a better attitude from her.

Finally, after a long struggle I felt, bit by bit, I was getting my daughter back. I did allow certain freedoms, though a little at a time. Like she was allowed to go to her sister's to see Harry and spend time with her little nephew, if she'd helped do jobs around the house. On a couple of occasions she was allowed to walk to her counselling session. Approximately, 15 minutes' walk away. (I must admit on those occasions, I watched the clock like a hawk, in case she'd never arrived or that she hadn't come straight back home). She didn't let me down. She had reached her destination and had also arrived back home promptly.

This had been an achievement in itself, I'd felt more positive about things turning a corner. Darcy and I had a trip to the bowling alley and we had thoroughly enjoyed it. As a rare treat for us we had a Kentucky Fried chicken meal together. Right out of the blue, Darcy suddenly said to me.

"You know what mum? I'm glad that you took my iPhone off me, I'm not bothered about it now and I no longer want it back. I'm so much happier without it."

What an outcome that was! I never want to feel like I've won. I only think Thank God for Darcy. I know it's been tough for her. I feel that during this period Darcy has grown up a little and I'm just relieved and as happy as she is, though I realized, it wouldn't last forever, as the teenage years are the worst, I feel we can look forward to sharing a closer relationship going forward.

I never count my chickens before they hatch, but I have to believe that this is the start of a new phase in both our lives.

STILL NO DEATH CERTIFICATE FOR MOLLY

Looking back now I'm no nearer getting closure. The months have passed by slowly. My mental health has suffered, due to everything which has happened. I'm still on prescription medication, which I might add, has little or no effect. The panic attacks kept on happening, when I least expect them.

Without the excellent team of friends, who have supported me, and who are still supporting me, I doubt I would have found the strength to go on. I've been seeing a Mental Health Counselor which has helped me, yet at the end of each session I end up feeling extremely low, having to keep going over everything is emotionally draining. Facing every aspect of myself and the family's lives is truly difficult, I'm having to recall each and every aspect of the trauma of my life and it's been debilitating. Nothing will ever bring Molly back I have continued to have the one recurring nightmare, one which, I can't comprehend or come to terms with.

Not very long ago I received a letter from the Burnley Borough Council demanding £600 in one letter then £400 in the next demand. These assessments were for non-payment of Community Tax, which they maintain were outstanding. I'm not a high paid earner, yet one after another arrears letters keep piling up. Like, I had also received a demand for rent arrears. Again I have always had a reduced rent, due to being a single parent and also my earnings are well below the national average. So, I do work, yes! I prefer to work even though my job as a cleaner only pays me a small amount of money per month, which amounts to not much more than £400 a month. How can it be right that I'm being chased for these extra costs? I'm doing my best but it's becoming impossible for me to carry on working.

Even after Molly died, after a month, I'd pushed myself to get back to working. I had needed to do something to stop me from going over the edge. I realized after the first anniversary of Molly's death I should have gone off sick, as my doctor had advised. Instead I had pushed and pushed myself in the wrong direction. It had possibly been the worst thing I could have done. I'd been bottled everything up, it's only now at this later stage some 14 months later, I had finally realized my body was getting closer and closer to a shut down.

It took me over 14 months to face clearing out Molly's belongings. I'd already decorated her bedroom and had left it in a neat a tidy order. Molly prided herself on tidiness, everything tidily put away. Her appearance had always been neat and immaculate. I had needed to take a deep breath before opening the wardrobe door. Every item of her clothes had a memory for me. I took one after the other down and laid them out. I'd sensed her presence, could see her in my mind's eye wearing each and every one of them.

It had been hard for me to do, as I hugged each of her dresses. Then, I'd wept as I picked out the one I had bought her for Christmas, with its label still intact. Sadly I never saw Molly wore it. That's when I had needed the strength to take hold of myself, before making a the hard decision to let go of them all and to decide which, of her two best friends, would like and suit, each item of clothing.

These two girls were the ones who had missed Molly the most, who had sent me the most text messages, even if it's only a quick hello are you okay message? They are so much appreciated by me.

Christmas, 2018 loomed in a foreboding way for me. Again it's not a time of year which brings joy to our family. Adam had settled down with a lovely girl and is doing his best to work through the sadness of losing his sister. His girlfriend, Olivia is a lovely caring person and someone I have become to like and love. She'd known and loved Molly too, therefore that being the case she was, possibly someone Adam had needed to help him deal with his sadness and this has continued in a positive way. With Olivia's support Adam, is doing his best to deal with his own emotions, I feel possibly that men find it hard to show their emotions. Adam, to us, is more or less the head of our small family he probably suffered the most, not knowing how to take away the pain for us or to be in a position to do much about it. I felt happy he's found someone to share his life with and this for me is a good sign.

With a lot of hardship and struggle I had managed to squirrel away some savings and had been able to secure a cheap offer on an all-inclusive holiday to Gran Canaria. Myself and Darcy are to spend Christmas, 2018 away from home. Last year, Christmas had been hard and had passed in a blur. Molly, of course is always with us in spirit throughout the year. Christmas, will always be the hardest time for me and will remain so. Being at home alone without her in our lives still hurts so much.

Many people who have lost a loved one would, also find it equally as hard as we all do. Some people turn to drink or drugs, trying to kill the pain of loss or even take their own lives. Of course, I too have relied heavily on prescription drugs, yet still had managed to hold on by forcing myself out of the house, keeping on working hard to keep the roof over our heads. The pain never leaves me, I only sleep with the nightly prescription of sleeping pills, which leave me feeling drowsy, but I could never have stayed home all day feeling morose and sad, I would almost certainly without doubt have caved in.

Listening to the music I love too, has helped enormously. One piece of music, especially comes to mind, by the Foo Fighters, the words I relate to so much it's called:

One of these days.'

One of these days the ground will drop out from beneath your feet

One of these days your heart will stop and play its final beat

One of these days the clocks will stop and time won't mean a thing

I have tried to think of a song each day to sum up how I've been feeling. It may seem a strange way of coping but it helps me to go on and get through my cleaning job. Medication slows me down, yet without it I couldn't have got out of bed in a morning. Then a panic attack strikes, and I am back to feeling lost and totally only my own in my own prison.

So much unhappiness hit my family the day Molly died. Even my little grandson Harry, cannot understand where she is. He's such a joy, he misses her too. I feel unable to cope on many days but I need to for the sake of him and the rest of the family.

The brightest shining star, however, during this time has to have been, Darcy. She had turned a negative into a positive. She had sorted out the bullies in the only way she could have done. Instead of being a target she then applied herself to the important things in life. She'd taken up boxing for self-protection.

For her birthday she'd received a keyboard and a guitar. Amazingly, she had taken to music like a natural performer. Her life is so different from what it had been six months ago. We still try to find time to do things together, which is precious. She has become a real treasure to me. It's been a long road for both of us, but at last there does appear to be a light at the end of the tunnel. Going forward I'm glad my perseverance and love for Darcy has turned both our lives around and I'm so thankful. I pray that this will continue, even though I realize the teen years are difficult, I want to believe we now have a better relationship with each other which I shall forever strive for, and is one of the reasons I will stay strong for my family.

We had organized a Spiritual Event, where Mick Magnem, the well-known and respected spiritualist would be attending to help us raise monies for the NHS Advocate, in aid of mental health. Sadly, one week before the meeting, the news reached us that Mick Magnem had died of a heart attack. Some wise spark said. *'I wonder if he saw that coming.'* Apparently, he was with a medical doctor at the time. Seemingly, despite a doctor being on hand the heart attack had proved to be fatal.

The organized meeting had obviously been cancelled. A few weeks later an event was arranged to raise funds for his widow. His wife had been left with three children to care for. Gail and myself, who had good reason to be part of this fund raiser, along with three of our Spiritualists who would be taking the stage had managed to draw in a large amount of people. A raffle was organized and altogether £700 was raised for his widow. Mick Magnem had given up his time freely for the Spiritual church. As a person he was well thought of and liked. He helped raise funds on many occasions at church for good causes. Even for MIND, which raised lots of money in Molly's name, which I know she would have supported after her experiences being sectioned under the mental health act.

The Inquest into Molly's death is well overdue, I have no Death Certificate for her. I need for Molly to be at rest, I've been told the Inquest is being delayed due to paperwork not being in place from the few private mental hospitals where Molly had been sectioned. The need to know is taking up so much time. What happened to her whilst in the care of these establishments? Too many questions which have not been addressed nor admitted to, as to why Molly had been given a certain drug? A drug which I have since learned, should never have been given to a person under the age of twenty years old, which applied to Molly.

The vast amount of paperwork involved in Molly's case is part of the reason it's taken so long due to her being sent from one hospital to another throughout her ordeal. Every aspect of her care has to go under a microscope to find out what caused Molly to take her own life. No stone will be left unturned until we get justice for her and to try to understand how, in this day and age, someone as young and vibrant like Molly would ever have considered taking her own life. She loved people too much and had so much to give. She had always said she didn't feel suicidal.

I will never rest until I get answers. I cannot move forward or feel better until somebody explains why she would have done such a thing. Something had gone badly wrong and I cannot accept she would have put her family through that kind of pain, it was simply not in her makeup.

So, now when I get home, I close the door at night, I feel locked in a place that nobody would want to be. I needed at all times to be left alone, never to have to speak to anyone again in my life. I sounds dramatic, yet all my true friends and people I hold close understand, let me know they care, even if I don't reply to them immediately. In my heart they keep me strong.

Darcy, her dad and I attended the last of Darcy's counselling sessions recently. As far as our relationship goes, it's been successful. Each of us had to write down what we hoped for the future for Darcy. Once the Counsellor had opened our hidden secrets, it turned out that we all wanted what was the best possible outcome for Darcy. We were both pleased after learning that Darcy had written something very similar to ours, which was great progress considering the journey she's been on. The fact that Darcy had to wait eight months to get this help had been abysmal, considering she had lost her sister in the way she had. Sudden, without warning, out of the blue, not expected. How does a child at thirteen years old deal with that kind of trauma.

When I look through the paperwork I've acquired between myself and Hazel, the Advocate who is working with me and the Ombudsman, I can see there is so much wrong with the system. Because of this, I have many ongoing issues to be addressed with regard to the lack or poor treatment available within the Mental Health care in this country. The lack of Counselors the continued denial of what goes on in the Mental Health wards in these establishments. Many of these treatments I have witnessed, I need to get answers from the people responsible. I will not rest until something is done more quickly for the people who need an immediate appointment and given the help they need when they need it.

A few nights ago a male friend of mine emailed me to say he had no friends and no reason to live. He said I was the only person who he could understand him and turned to me in his hour of need. Well, that kind of sums up what I've been trying to say for months. That night he killed himself after being told it be six months before he could see anyone. Once again I am devastated, this is just another of many suicide happening somewhere every day of the week. I rest my case!

GETTING THROUGH CHRISTMAS 2018

Christmas for our family will never be the same since losing Molly. Christmas is the time of year when families generally get together and celebrate. It was very difficult last year and for me and Christmas will always be the time of year that breaks my heart, knowing Molly will never be with the family again. It was hard but I did have to put aside my own feelings for my grandson's sake. Harry is only five years old and can't possibly be expected to feel the same pain as we all do. Because of that we did plan a small party prior to Christmas when all the family got together and we did our best to make it a happy time for him giving him his Christmas presents and joining in his excitement.

Although Harry does remember Molly and still talks about her, on occasions, he points to the sky and says 'Molly's up there'. He cannot comprehend, or understand how our lives have changed, nor should he, he's only a small child and it's perfectly normal that he should have a Christmas like any other young child at this time of year.

People may have thought that because I'd booked the whole of the Christmas week away with Darcy, we would be off on a jolly holiday. Nothing could have been further from the truth. Both of us had stayed at home last year and this year we felt in need of a restful time away from Burnley and to recharge our batteries ready for another year, hopefully, one without conflict.

Even though, Darcy and I had helped others by spending the whole of Christmas Day 2017, at the food bank. It had helped us more, to be honest, keeping our hands and minds busy to make other people's Christmas a festive time with a meal and presents. It did help us to feel we'd done something good and it also helped us to get through the Christmas period. Sadly, wishing it would be over as quickly as possible. Not that we wanted to forget Molly as she is in my heart every day of the year, it's just so much harder at Christmas for us all.

So, this year we were not going away to the sun to party. For Darcy it was a treat to help her put aside all the trauma of being bullied and still missing Molly. For me, I just wanted to get as far away from home and try to recharge my batteries to help me get through the next twelve months as I know there are still many issues not resolved as yet. It's taking forever for the inquest to be held in respect of Molly and for us to finally get a death certificate. Until this happens I am unable to put her and my mind to rest.

As it turned out the hotel I had booked for us was in the middle of nowhere, it was at least a two miles walk to get down to the beach area We had an amazing view of the sea from our balcony and it was certainly a haven of peace, I loved just sitting there staring out, allowing the peace of this idyllic place to wash over me.

Thankfully, our room was almost up in the clouds and well away from the activities going on in the main hotel reception area and I must admit I only ventured down mainly for meals, occasionally to walk or find a spot where it was quiet and peaceful. Or for Darcy's sake we'd try to find sun beds away from the pool area if possible.

By night time, after eating our evening meal, I felt unable to join in with the merry makers. In fact, I suffered from a few panic attacks and felt I had needed to return to the bedroom where I did spend many hours alone there. Thankfully, Darcy, at fourteen years old now, was capable and sensible enough to find herself a couple of friends to spend time with. Yet, she always popped back to the room from time to time to see me and never stayed downstairs watching the entertainment until late. Some of the time we'd spend together on the balcony reading books and generally keeping ourselves to ourselves. Although the hotel offered everything I could wish for, it couldn't take away the loss for me, letting her down.

A NEW YEAR BEGINS - 2019

I had wished in my heart that January 2019 may bring some joy and hope.

Having to go to my January counselling session was very much what I needed. I could confide my inner most thoughts and explain that my anxiety level had been at its height whilst I'd was away. The panic attacks had been intense and indescribably, it is impossible to explain the intensity of pain. The thought of leaving the bedroom and facing people was terrifying. It may sound incredulous having travelled there by plane and having found a small piece of paradise in a most beautiful resort to spend quiet time there. It was unbelievably hard for me to relax, I felt totally out of my depth. Yet when I thought about it, all of the past years worry and troubles had built up and had put me in a place I felt I couldn't escape from. It's not easy to explain unless you've ever had such attacks; it's difficult to stop it happening in fact it's impossible to keep them from happening.

My counsellor questions me endlessly and listens to everything I say and just being there is worth so much to me. She helps me to understand and to help me deal with things in a more constructive way. Though, I must admit, I don't think that time will come any time soon.

Facing yet more reminder letters, for back rent and council tax arrears I'm supposed to owe, is one of the many things I have to deal with on my own. I do not owe this money, I have never been in debt, and I've always managed to pay all the bills on time. This was the reason I had made the decision to go out to work and not to have to rely on benefits.

However, it now appears in order to conform to all the rules about benefits etc., I'm informed I would be far better off if I go on Universal Credit. *WHAT!* How can that be the right way to go? It's totally beyond my understanding. All I tried to do was not claim money off anyone and make my own way in life, yet the system seems to be making life as difficult as they can for people who want to work. Of course, I've appealed and I've a lovely person called Lindsay, who knows the system, and how it works, I have to believe that eventually all these outstanding invoices, bills, requests amounting to somewhere in the region of £2,000 + interest for non-payment will cease to drop through my letterbox. It does make me wonder how I will ever be able to recover my state of mind with all this stuff surfacing and causing me even more grief.

Perhaps because of, or maybe it has contributed to my state of health, I've recently been diagnosed with Post Traumatic Stress. (Bit of a pun that post bit). Strange to give it that name to be honest but finally I've had to admit defeat and have to agree it is the only option I have to apply for the Universal Credit. Maybe I should have done this many months ago and given myself time to heal instead of running around like a headless chicken trying to earn a living. Once I'm feeling the benefit of not having to work long hours maybe I will begin to live again.

I'm honestly hoping my patience will return and I will stop feeling out of control. The not sleeping or living on sleeping pills and generally going through life like a robotic nomad makes my life hell. These symptoms I'm informed are all part of the PTS syndrome caused by everything life has thrown at me, not just recently, but for my whole life. Trying to cope with far too many things has finally caused my body to shut down. I know I shall rise again. I know deep inside myself I'm a very strong person and I shall survive no matter what. I still have a lot to achieve yet and also the more pressing matter is getting justice for Molly. I will always fight and be strong for my family who mean everything to me and who knows there may still be hope for the future that life and happier days will come, I have to believe it will.

There have been some slightly comforting good moments or signs that things were slowly moving on at times. Like Darcy, who I feel so proud of, she has shown great strength and maturity with regards to the bullying at school. Despite all of that she has now gone on to do well in the boxing classes she attends it has given her so much more confidence. Her school work has been given the thumbs up by her teachers and she had achieved high marks and good comments from all. It also appears she's a natural when it comes to music since being given the keyboard for her birthday and surprised us all by immediately taking to it and can now play many pieces.

So, things have begun to turn a small corner. Looking back I'm amazed, when comparing the situation since last year. There are some things which are still ongoing, yet other things with respect to family have been encouraging. All this has helped me to some extent. That is, of course, until I receive the next demand letters which, continually pop through the letter box which reminds me things are still not perfect but 'm always hopeful life will start to feel better.

Adam and Olivia are now become a real couple now and that has surprised and delighted me. Of course, Olivia was one of Molly's loveliest and kindest friends, she was the one who was there for Molly the night she became ill and which is mentioned earlier on in the book. Olivia had stuck by our family throughout Molly's illness and her tragic death.

I could not have been happier when Adam and Olivia became friends initially, and I think a good match. In some ways I have always regarded Olivia as a God send and I don't say that lightly. She has remained a rock to me and has been unbelievably understanding and caring towards Adam who, I know has had to survive the pain and devastation of losing his lovely sister. Olivia has supported him and helped him to deal with his emotions and finally they have decided to make a go of it and I couldn't be more pleased. Who could have understood how Adam was feeling better than Olivia, who had been so loyal to us as a she would her own family?

Even though I was pretty sure Olivia was pregnant, when they announced it a few weeks ago, I was pleased for them. The baby is due in August this year and they told me if the baby is a girl they will be naming her Rosie Molly which I was so touched by. It's at times like this when I get news I would happening to us as a family, happy things and that's the way, I'm praying that will continue to happen. I have to begin to look forward and feel more positive. It will be hard for me but I've a feeling that once we get to the truth of Molly's death I may just be able to start to always think, I must tell Molly the news then realise she's no longer with us, but, perhaps she is in spirit. Sadly this kind of thing brings me back down to earth when the realisation hits home that I will never be able to share my joy or sadness or even a conversation with her ever again.

I must admit though that things do seem to be slowly turning the corner and appear to be improve over the coming year. Until then I shall do my level best to get myself well and try to believe there will be a brighter future. Molly loved and spoilt Harry, she loved kids, unfortunately she will never get the chance to hold the new baby and love him/her, but I know for sure she would've been so happy for Olivia and Adam. Oh, and I've got another snippet of news Harry's mum, Katie has recently got herself a job at Asda cafe, she's thrilled to bits.

This time last year I'd made the decision not to go back to the Spiritual Church, I still was unable to believe, at that time, there was a God and have felt like a lost soul for such a long time since. Slowly and gradually I've returned to the church to do some cleaning for them. I do support all the good things they do and have at times helped with the fund raising events which raise money for deserving causes, and I do get involved at those times, yet I'm not sure if my faith will ever return, I do feel the warmth from the people at the Spiritual Church who have all been kind and comforting to me over the many months, maybe just maybe I will slowly return but I do feel the love and perhaps this is another positive sign. I have to believe going forward; I cannot keep feeling this anger in me day after day I really have to find my way back to a safer place.

I've lost count of the times I've looked up and spotted a little robin in the back garden, it makes me smile. Sometimes I'll find a penny in the street or see a white feather floating by every now and then. I do question these signs, my faith, and whether these signs are sent from heaven to give me peace of mind. It always leaves me feeling close to Molly, at this time which is good.

MOVING AWAY FROM SPIRITUAL CHURCH

This time last year I'd made the decision not to go back to the Spiritual Church, I still was unable to believe, at that time, there was a God and have felt like a lost soul for such a long time since. Slowly and gradually I've returned to the church to do some cleaning for them. I do support all the good things they do and have at times helped with the fund raising events which raise money for deserving causes, and I do get involved at those times, yet I'm not sure if my faith will ever return, I do feel the warmth from the people at the Spiritual Church who have all been kind and comforting to me over the many months, maybe just maybe I will slowly return but I do feel the love and perhaps this is another positive sign. I have to believe this, going forward; I cannot keep feeling this anger in me day after day I really have to find my way back to a safer place.

I've lost count of the times I've looked up and spotted a little robin in the back garden, it makes me smile. Sometimes I'll find a penny in the street or see a white feather floating by every now and then. I do question these signs, my faith, and whether these signs are sent from heaven to give me peace of mind. It always leaves me feeling close to Molly, which is good.

I'm honestly hoping my patience will return and I will stop feeling out of control. The not sleeping or living on sleeping pills and generally going through life as a robotic nomad. These things I'm informed are all part of the PTS syndrome with everything life has thrown at me over many months and trying to cope with far too many things my body practically shut down. I shall rise again, I know I'm a very strong person and I shall always keep pressing on until I get full justice for Molly and fight to help all my family to learn to live and perhaps enjoy living once more.

There are some slight moments when things feel like they are moving on. Seeing Darcy doing well at her boxing class, also her school work has been given the thumbs up by her teachers, she has done well this year, despite the bullies. She's a natural when it comes to music and has surprised us with her musical talents on the keyboard she received for her birthday. So things are beginning to turn a small corner. All these things help me to some extent until the next demand letter pops through the letter box to drag me down once more.

THE BABY IS BORN

Sadly my health over the last few months had deteriorated to the extent I'd suffered daily from panic attacks. I had blinding headache's and a lack of strength trying to adjust to the loss of Molly. Of course, it goes without saying that Molly is always on my mind and her death hit me as hard as it would any mother who loved her child. I'd taken a step back, I'd have to stop running around like a headless chicken, and simply take all the time off I needed to cope better with life.

For a long time it was a struggle and my account of these months is a blur but I needed to find a way out of feeling this terrible pain in my heart. It had helped a lot in the knowledge, that very soon Olivia would be giving birth to their

It had helped a lot in the knowledge, that very soon Olivia would be giving birth to their first child and of course, I was as excited to hear about their hopes and plans for the new baby. The expected date of birth had been given as middle to end of August 2019, as with all births no-one could predict the exact date. So, when Olivia was due to go for her final check-up prior to the birth in August, she'd asked me to go along with both Adam and herself to the hospital. I was happy to be included. In fact, Olivia had wanted me there for a special reason. Once the gender of the child was known, Olivia only wanted me to know. She'd asked the nurse only to divulge to me whether it was a boy or girl and no-one else, and that I should keep it secret until the upcoming baby shower in late July when the BIG reveal was to be announced in front of all family and friends present on that day. I'd also been asked to buy one of these new fire crackers which, when activated, would shower the room with room with a pink or blue confetti.

Most of our family were to meet for the first time with Olivia's parents and her aunties and uncles. It was certainly a day full of love and fun. We were made so welcome at Adam and Olivia new home, which had a super sun area at the rear, where we could mix and chat until I was to hand over the cracker to Adam who would announce the true identity of the baby. I passed the cone shaped cracker to Adam and everyone waited anxiously to see what the explosion would reveal.

Four or five attempts later and finally, Olivia had to come to the rescue to show Adam how to activate the cracker correctly, which had made everyone laugh loudly, and at last the cracker went off with a bang filling the room in shower of blue confetti then, at last, everyone clapped and whooped at the news. All the presents were then opened and Olivia looked flushed and happy with all the beautiful things people had so kindly brought with them. For me, I believe it was possibly the first time I can remember laughing and feeling the warmth of such a close-knit family I was so happy for both of them.

Not long after the reveal party Olivia, goes into labour.

One of the biggest joys in life is when a baby is born. Adam and Olivia are such proud parents of Ollie, he's a beautiful child. As promised, they've named him Ollie. He is so welcome, the cutest little baby, ever. He does look like his daddy, but he's the most adorable and pleasant child, loved by all of us, he has brought a much-needed love and joy to all our lives.

CHRISTMAS 2019 AND NEW YEAR 2020

For the second year in a row, I'd booked Darcy and myself into a hotel for the Christmas week in the Canaries. I had believed that by going away it would take away the pain of losing Molly. Of course, that hadn't been the case. When Christmas Eve arrived, there I was again, sobbing my heart out thinking about Molly, feeling that she should have been here with us, exactly the same scenario as the previous two Christmases. It was becoming a vigil to my missing child, my escape route. Having sat there for over an hour I'd stopped for a moment, I made my way out of the sliding glass doors and on to the balcony. What on earth had I been doing for the past three years, there away from home and still I'm not feeling any better. Nothing had changed.

My youngest daughter, Darcy, had become my career, not only that she'd had to fend for herself. Every night she'd go off alone, down into the entertainments area and had made friends with one or two teenagers of similar age who, let her join them. That had been due to my inability to go with her, I'd felt a terrible panic attacks and my heart would thud in my chest. I simply was not equipped to be a part of the hotel's jolly Christmas festivities. We would always have our evening meal together, though.

What kind of a mum had I become to her? In my grief, despite having taken my prescribed medication for anxiety, I'd simply become dependent on Darcy. I'd needed to lean on her. Surely, this year I had needed to step up and become the mother I should be. I'd started to feel bad about having let her down, all this time I'd not been there for her.

Darcy had turned fifteen back in September of last year. This should have been the start of her young adolescent years, a time to feel free and to enjoy this time of her life: she should not have had to struggle on her own. Darcy had enjoyed parts of all the holidays we'd been on at Christmastime. Yet, it had taken me all this time to realise there had been a role reversal in our relationship. She surely must have resented having to look after me. Of course, she too, had been going through the same emotions as I had, having lost her sister. Thinking about it now, it does explain some of her angry outburst, I'd put it down to her age, she must have felt like shouting at me for not realising, that, in my sorrow, she'd needed me more, she was alive, not dead. Now, as I think back, I must have, unintentionally, made her feel invisible.

I'd finally started to think long and hard about my life. Not just my life, but what I'd been putting everyone through. I couldn't see beyond my own grief. I'd sunk into a hole, a hole I could not climb out off, I couldn't let go of Molly.

It had been time to start to take stock and as the thought struck me things took a turn.

I'd started to talk out loud to myself.

'What the hell are you doing thousands of miles away from your family, Karen, especially, at Christmastime?'

For the first time in three years, I'd at last realised I had to put things into perspective. I'd been totally thinking of my own reasons for getting far away at Christmas, and by taking Darcy away from her family and friends back home at this time of year, had been wrong. We should've all been together, not thousands of miles apart.

For the first time since we had arrived I'd opened my eyes, saw through the glare of bright and beautiful day, that life had to be lived. Shielding my eyes, I'd looked around and saw clearly what a truly peaceful place we were staying in. Gardens stretched around the hotel, flowers in a mixture of reds and yellow blooms swayed in a gentle breeze. Beneath the balcony I could see the amazing pool area, where people were relaxing. Kiddies were laughing joyously, jumping in and out of the pool, and I was alone just looking down on it all not being a part of it.

This, I believe had been the turning point. I'd felt, at peace. I'm not sure what had happened to me, but I'd decided in that moment something had to change, I'd needed to do something positive. I'd returned to the room, had picked up my mobile phone, and fired off a message, to my son, Adam. With tears blurring my vision, I had managed to text a one line message, and had posted it. *'Adam, what the hell are we doing here? Being away from you all, at Christmas?* His one-liner, returned immediately. *'We feel the same, mum.'*

From that day on, I knew my mind set had changed, it simply had been time to let go for my own sanity and I'd to make things right, for Darcy. That following day we'd been up and out of bed and downstairs for an early breakfast and had beaten the German's to the sun-beds, claiming a great position, poolside. I'd had a lot to make up to Darcy, and I had wanted to make sure Darcy would have my full attention. I had done my utmost to assure her how much I loved her, had made her feel special, she'd needed to know how much I cared about her. In my mind, as I'd sat there looking at my lovely girl.

I'd realised how much we had needed each other and for me that had been the new start we had needed. I'd needed to show the love to Darcy to thank her for all she'd done. We'd both missed out on so much in recent times, but most of all I need to keep on telling her, I do and did always love her, and I need to remind myself every day to prove that to her.

On that first day by the pool, we had joined a group of people who had been playing water sports. I'd grabbed a tight hold of Darcy's hand and we'd jumped into the pool together. It had been great fun and for a time and we'd both started to relax and had enjoyed ourselves. Once I'd exhausted myself and had stepped out of the pool, I'd managed to encourage a nice young lad to take over from me in the pool. It had ended up that Darcy had found herself a mate for the rest of the week. At last, the clouds of sorrow had taken a back seat for both of us, that day and for the first time in a long time, I'd felt like we were a team, a mother and daughter team, again.

Darcy had spent time out with her new friend. I'd been happy for her. I'd love to see how her eyes glowed, and how full of life she was. My little girl was growing up fast, and it had made me feel so good.

It had been a sad parting when we'd had to leave for home. Darcy' had tears in her eye as they'd said their goodbyes. Her new best friend lived a little too far away, in the Midlands. Once they were both back to their respective homes, they had sent text messages between each other, but like any holiday romance it had since fizzled out, she'd moved on and was back in school.

Getting through January had been hard. I'd a lot of issues to work through, most of my past life, to be honest.

I'd needed to find a new mind set. A lot of my time, during January had been taken up with my parents. They have been my *rocks*, throughout my life. They have never judged me or made me feel unloved. I had to face the fact that my lovely mum had begun to show signs of dementia. Her memory had become dreadful. I would ask her when my birthday was and she'd struggled to think, let alone get it correct. We did laugh a little tough, when dad had mentioned she'd sent everyone two Christmas cards.

It needs to be said that my dad got us all through all the bad times and well as the good. He's got an amazing sense of humour. He'd been taking care of all of us for so many years, especially me! Nowadays, dad's time is constantly taken up by looking after my mum. For many years he's got me and my children through crisis after crisis. His heart and my mother's heart had been broken, as too my children's. Over the nineteen years of Molly's life my mother and dad had been mother and father, granddad and grandma to her. They had nurtured her so much throughout her childhood and teenage years: she'd been so close to them both of them. All my children respect and loved them too. For Molly though, she'd clung to them the most, had needed them the most, they were devastated and I don't think they will ever get over the death of Molly.

THE FINAL INQUEST OF MOLLY CARTER

February,2020 had arrived. I needed to get myself together for the upcoming Inquest regarding what had happened to my daughter. Evidence was to be given on the cause of death, and more importantly, I did need answers to the many questions, which had run through my mind over and during the last three years. I had been informed that the Inquest was to be held in Blackburn as opposed to Burnley, on the 24 February 2020.

Prior to that date, my solicitor had contacted me to finalise the paperwork to take with us to the Inquest. Adam had gone along with me to hear how they thought the hearing would go. We had listened to them for over an hour. On leaving their office, both my son and I, had felt the same ominous premonition, that we would not be getting a fair outcome as to what had happened or that certain specialists doctors would not be at the Inquest to be questioned about the seriousness of the treatment Molly had received during her time at the Cygnet Mental Health Care in Bradford.

My solicitors had explained to us what the inquest would entail. He'd explained this was not a court, in the normal way of things, like having a judge and jury. It wouldn't be a name blaming exercise. It was the normal procedure to bring witnesses to court. The many people who had treated Molly throughout her illness, those who had been responsible for her care during the time she had been hospitalised. We were led to believe evidence would be forthcoming regarding the medication Molly had been prescribed, which to me, was a major concern. Throughout the time Molly had spent at the Cygnet Health Care hospital in Bradford, we had many concerns about her treatment, especially a particular drug she had been prescribed. Which, at a much later stage, we were to learn, should not have been administered to Molly due to her age at that time.

We'd needed answers, we needed to know who had authorised and prescribed this medication. We needed that person to come forward at the inquest to stand up and to explain why Molly had been put on this drug. We needed to hear that person apology, or to at least get the specialist doctor to admit he'd prescribed a wrong drug, which we do believe had a lot to do with why Molly became so ill. A mistake had been made, there's no doubt at all about this, it's in the evidence. A mistake had been made and myself, and my family needed someone to admit this to us, she'd been put into a comatose state, and that as far as we were concerned, was inexcusable.

Molly had been moved around a lot due to shortages of beds and in all she'd spent time in round five different locations. Apparently, we'd been advised the actual outcome of the inquest It had probably already been decided by the Coroner, prior to the Inquest date. We are told the witnesses were only there to give their account of what had happened. The outcome was to decide what actually happened throughout the many weeks she'd spent in mental institutions. The final outcome had to be made as to why Molly had taken her own life, whether she'd been of sound mind. It has been well documented by me in this book earlier on, and therefore, I will not be labouring the points already spoken about in this book. However, what we were to see and hear over the three days period was, in our opinion, a complete cover up.

We all attended, Adam, Olivia his partner, my dad and a friend of mine, Sarah.

Day one began - everyone was seated before the Coroner. Our Solicitor was present, the witnesses who included two doctors two nurses, Molly's Boy Friend, Kristen, during the time she was incarcerated. And of course, Patrick, Molly's Caret who I have repeatedly, mentioned throughout the book. Patrick, who had been Molly's qualified Social Worker and a qualified Care Coordinator. He'd had years of experience working with young people.

Of course, every court case takes a long time to go through, so I will not give a line by line account of what and who the witnesses were. A Solicitor had been representing The Cygnet Private Mental Care Centre at Bradford, to report on the major care issue, which led up to Molly's death. That, of course, was in connection as to who had prescribed a medication known as Zuclopenhixol, which she should never have been given. It appeared no-one was admitting anything in respect of that. However, it was a drug she was prescribed during her time at this mental health establishment. Yet no-one had been forthcoming as to who had prescribed this medication for her. No one under the age of 20 years of age should have been given this drug. Molly was nineteen years old when she entered the Cygnet Mental Care in Bradford.

I'd realised, not long after the inquest had opened, we would not be getting to the bottom of why my daughter took her own life. Day one, I sobbed throughout the hearing having to listen to everyone's account. I listened in utter disbelief as one after the other was sworn in and nothing was forthcoming with regard to Molly's treatment.

Finally, I had been called and had to be sworn in. As I faced the Coroner, I'd had gone into a stare upwards, into the middle space behind the Coroner's head. Through my blurred teary eyes all I could see in that empty space, had been that terrifying image of Molly, that memory, which haunts me to this day, when I'd put the key in the lock, walked into the hallway, and had seen my beautiful girl, hanging. This terrible tragedy will stay in my mind forever, whatever the outcome of this inquest, I go away from here without my daughter and without the result I was hoping for.

I'd felt numb throughout this inquest. I'd felt it was an absolute mockery, an insult to my Molly. This inquest would not be giving me or my family the peace of mind or the result we'd tried so hard for. The truth as to what, or who had been responsible for Molly's early discharge or the truth behind the wrong medication, or even to have treated her better, when she was in such a vulnerable state. She had pleaded, begged, she'd been beside herself with anxiety and in pain the night before. She'd asked for help, the help was needed right then. Not the day after. The day after, Molly was to take her own life. Nobody ever believed she would've ever have done this and even now I still do not know what had gone through her mind. She'd always said when asked. 'Do you feel suicidal,' Molly without fail always replied with a clear voice 'No' she'd never thought of suicide.

I'd known from that day forward the inquest into Molly's death would produce no answers for us. I'd known we would never get the truth behind what really happened to Molly, throughout the time she was away from us, I still believe that the reason behind Molly taking her own life had been partly due to incorrect medication she was given, which no-body would take responsibility for. Paperwork had been lost, and her care throughout her stay in Bradford broke my heart. These factors, I totally believe led to her death. I'd gone to the Inquest, to fight for her, to get to the truth. All we heard from many of the sworn in witnesses was mainly lies to protect themselves. In my family's opinion it was like a Kangaroo Court. Almost every one of them pointed the finger at Patrick.

On day two, more witnesses had given their account of what had happened. It struck me as a little strange, that almost all of them had been at pains to blame Patrick totally for Molly's death. I had written so much in my book about Patrick, about how I thought he had let us down, yet there had been so many other people involved in her care, and who had played as much a part as Patrick, throughout the many weeks, months, Molly had been treated badly and at that moment. I could barely look at Patrick. I had, of course, thought we'd been let down by him too. Yet, there were so many others who could have done more, who could have come forward.

A doctor from Bradford, who had been called as a witness from Cygnet Metal Health Care in Bradford, had, on oath, the audacity to say he used to sit with the patients whilst they ate their food. For Molly, this was untrue, he was trying to give the impression he known Molly personally and had looked after her in a caring manner. In my opinion, it was anything but the truth. I'd felt like jumping out of my seat, I felt I needed to shout out that he was telling lies and had sat on my hands to stop myself from doing something I might regret. Finally, I had to resign myself; I would have to suffer in silence.

The fact is Molly had been taking the drug Zuclopenthixol since leaving The Cygnet Clinic and had continued being given this drug but was given a lower dose of this drug whilst spending time at the Harbour Mental Health facility in Blackpool.

It was disgusting that nobody had been called to give evidence on this serious matter. It had been vital to the inquest that someone should have come forward to answer to us, her family. The allegation about the very strong medication which was prescribed for Molly in Bradford and the drug she was still in her system up to her taking her own life. It needed a specialist doctor from the Cygnet Clinic, to explain to us who had actually given her this medication. Nobody was prepared to tell us who that person had been was shameful that no-one was there to give out some information and/or an explanation. This, in our opinion, was a critical part of the evidence, and needed to be examined by our Solicitor. We firmly believe and will continue to believe this drug had been a contributory factor in her taking her own life, due to the side effects of this medication.

Patrick, Molly's Care Coordinator had been the last witness called to the stand and had been sworn in. I don't think I've ever seen a man look so frail, and traumatised, as Patrick had. After being sworn in, he almost collapsed, he only uttered a few words before he totally broke down. He said

'I begged the doctor to come out, to see Molly that night.'

Tears ran down his face, he was obviously, extremely upset. Although he did try to make a point about the medication Molly had been prescribed and why had that information been intentionally dismissed. Then the Coroner returned his comments saying:

'Are you qualified to question a senior doctor's professional decision on medication?

I didn't know what to think. This had been the first time I'd set eyes on Patrick since the day before Molly had died. To see him so distressed up there, it did appear that Patrick had done something. I had to think about that for a time. This ordeal being on the stand had left Patrick in a complete emotional state. He'd slumped forward, sobbing his heart out. I honestly did not know how to feel. And I had absolutely no idea as to what had happened to him?

He'd looked like he'd lost a lot of weight, since I'd last seen him. That had been the last night when Molly had begged him to help her. Little did I know, just what had actually happened to Patrick, from that day he'd left my home, back in August 2017? I would discover, only a matter of weeks after the inquest, that something dreadful had occurred, which had not come out at the inquest.

The final outcome of the Inquest ruled 'Misadventure'. I had to accept the verdict. Molly had not left any notes to say she had intended to kill herself, so the result was probably the only result we could have got. It was, at last over, but I left with a heavy heart.

As we made our way out of the court we headed toward the stairwell. I had glanced downwards to the lower floors. I was furious to see Molly's biological father making his way out. I'd needed to scream all day. I had shouted at the top of my voice.

'What the fuck are you doing here?'

As he'd looked up in horror he slipped and fell. It was all I could do not to laugh out loud, the useless waste of space. He'd never been a father to Molly, never spent a penny on her or paid any maintenance. He didn't even know his own daughter. I can't tell you how terrible it made me feel to see such a moron turning up at the Inquest. It goes without saying, Molly never knew him, she'd not even recognise him if she'd ever seen him. He was nothing to her, only another person in her life, who totally let her down.

WE WELCOME PATRICK BACK TO OUR HOME

On our way home in the car, my dad had seemed quiet. Then he said to me. 'I'm going to ring Patrick up, tomorrow. That was a terrible ordeal he's gone through. I think we should find out perhaps what did happen to him after he'd left that day.'

My dad has always been a fair man, and I thought he was probably right in that, maybe he should get in touch with Patrick. He'd always liked him and thought him to be a kindly man. I too, had a need to know the truth about what had happened to him.

A couple of days later dad related to me what he'd found out, to be honest I was mortified. Like most people would be on hearing just what had gone on, and how Patrick almost suffered a heart attack by the nastiness he encountered the day he went back into work.

The receptionist and his boss sniggered when he walked in. (the two of them who had been called as witnesses at Molly's inquest). That day he'd gone back to his place of work, his boss had whispered in his ear.

'Hope you're records are up to date, Patrick. Molly hanged herself.'

Patrick had known he'd done everything he could have done. He'd left an urgent email online, for the office to pick up the follow morning and act on it. This was customary and was the first thing which was checked on a daily basis. The urgent ones had to be dealt with as urgent. Nobody got anyone to go to see Molly the day she committed suicide.

Patrick always checked in at his place of work. That day as he made his way to his own office, he had the shock of his life. What he saw was dreadful. He found a blow-up doll had been placed across his desk, where a note had left by the side of it. It was a grossly lewd and disgusting message, which was totally out of order. The fact that someone who has never admitted they had been responsible or had been capable of such gross behaviour.

After speaking with Patrick myself, I'd learned so much more from him and then he came over to see me so we'd spent a good number of hours together going over things.

Apparently, the blow-up doll had been put there by somebody. After this awful experience, Patrick decided to take the NHS Trust to a tribunal for bullying and did win his case. Patrick told us how his life had changed. He told me he'd left the office, voluntarily, he'd not been dismissed it had been his own decision, and he'd never returned. He told us it was certainly not the way he had ever anticipated leaving the job he'd worked a lifetime in, and one where he tried to make a difference.

My family will always welcome Patrick into our homes, we'd felt he had done right by Molly. Until the inquest we were totally in the dark as to what had happened to him. All we have since heard has put an absolutely different light on the awful matter, which changed our opinion about Patrick. How could the people he worked with have been allowed to have done such a disgraceful nasty trick on Patrick? He did not deserve that. Lies had been told and the appointment which Patrick believed had been allocated for Molly, had in fact, been allocated to another patient. He totally believed on that day Molly would be seen - in his mind he had checked in at reception on his arrival to work that morning, and had been told by reception there was a doctor slot available that day, which he rightly believed had been allocated to Molly as she did need an 'urgent care' appointment, due to side effects of the medication she'd been prescribed.

Therefore, Patrick did was he had always done and sent off an email message believing this would be pick up and dealt with immediately, the following morning. Nobody, it appears seems to have admitted to anything. His message had, obviously, not been dealt with. This surely had to have had a detrimental effect on Molly life. She never received so much as an urgent phone call. Or a call from that department and there had been no visits from a doctor or any other party on Molly's behalf in connection with the mental health team dealing with her case. The whole account of this matter, as to what had happened to Patrick, who by that time, had taken the matter further and went on to prove his case at a tribunal. This case was due to be published, but due to the lockdown in connection with Corvid19, it never got aired.

However, despite Patrick's article not being published, someone had contacted me from the Daily Mirror, they had asked for my reaction in connection to the outcome of the inquest. The gentleman who interviewed me, at length, at my home address stayed for well over an hour. He was eager to hear more about what had happened in respect of Molly, and he was a lovely kind and caring reporter. The following press article had been printed the following week. I thought at this juncture I should perhaps include this at the tail end of this book. If it helps anyone out there, who are at the mercy of bullies or who are suffering mental health issues, as Molly had. Then I pray they get help and stop suffering from people who bully, or people who post nasty social media or text messages, they really must find the help they need. There is always someone they could turn to or speak to.

TIME TO PUT MY LIFE IN ORDER

I'd had many sessions of therapy over the last few years. I believed that the time would come when I would have to face my demons, and to question my past. In my own words, to face up to the life I'd led.

The people who I'd thought had been my true friends. In fact, had not been my friends. I shouldn't have been hanging about on the street. It's taken me over 40 years to have realised that, because of my own choice to truant from school, to live a life with street kids was absolutely down to me. Somehow, it had formed the greater part of the of the person I would become in life, and how far I would slip down the wrong side of life ending up being totally out of control for most part of my childhood years. Not to mention most of my teenage years. I had still gone my own way down the path of recklessness. That way of life had still continued, I had chosen to carry on truanting from school, and continued to get into many dare devil situations.

Today, I sincerely want my parents to know what brilliant parents they've been. How sorry I am for putting them through what must, at times, have been heart breaking for them. I want them to read this and to know how truly sorry I am. I had no-one to blame but myself. I'd been too young, I'd been easily led, yet I had known right from wrong, and still my mind set carried on being a total let down to my parent.

I see clearly after all these years, that most of the people I'd hung about with had been a lot older than me, It had been easy for me, to be led astray, I believed because of my rebelliousness, and becoming a part of a what I'd thought was an exciting life had been more appealing to me than going to school. The truth is, it was wrong, and I'm not proud of the life I led.

On looking back, it must have been obvious to everyone else, but myself, that I was going further downhill, By the time I'd met the person I was to marry I'd realised, I'd found out to my cost, that I had made another bad choice. Somehow, my life was going worse. There's no turning the clock back in life, nothing can be done to undo the bad things, or bad decisions. The one thing I will never regret is having my four children, I would turn the world upside down for them, and I have at times. Somehow I was on a slippery course. Life hits you hard at times. Things don't always go the way you'd like them to go. All I can do is to go move on and try to become the best person I can be and try to live a happier and more contented life.

I'm am not proud of a lot of the things I've done, but now I've to try to move on, hopefully. There have been so many kind people who have befriended me since Molly's death. Good people, people, I never knew existed. I'm slowly but surely leaving behind those who I used to trust and today I'm moving forward, my past is over, I've never tried to hide the bad parts of my life, I've tried to be as truthful as I could be. I feel it's time for me to make changes, and to start living the rest of my life, only in a different way. It has taken a long time for me to accept I've made mistakes and now I need to change my ways and to make big changes, especially for my children, I've always loved my kids, I've worked hard to bring them up the best way I could, having been a single mum for many years. Adam and Katie both have a child to bring up and Darcy has the ability to do well and get whatever she wants out of life. They're everything and more to me and have always will be.

THE DAILY MIRROR PRINTS THE OUTCOME OF THE STORY

As previously mentioned a week after the Inquest I had been approached by The Daily Mirror newspaper. A few days later the press release went out and I was able to see the full extent of the report, which they had written after my interview with their reporter. He had wanted to know more about Molly as a person and what had happened during her short life. The reporter had put me at my ease and I had found him a kind and friendly interviewer, I had needed closure but I also wanted people to know what had happened after the inquest had ended.

As this published article is connected to my life story I'd felt the story of Molly should be published in that, I felt I needed to get the message out there and perhaps help others. Even if the message only gets through to one person, if it helps people to start being kind to each other. They may think twice about what the consequences are. Social Media has a lot to answer for. Bullying not only happens at school it continues long after the school gates close. If just one person survives, because of what happened to Molly, I would be grateful to have been a part of getting this message out there.

The final outcome of the Inquest had been 'Misadventure' so I had to accept the findings of this hearing. No matter what the outcome had been it would never have brought Molly back. I did feel I'd let her down with regards to getting justice for her. She'd died unnecessarily, her death could have been prevented and without doubt the truth of what happened to my daughter lies behind closed doors. I did my best, I could do no more.

The following extract is from The Daily Mirror Newspaper: -

THE MIRROR PRINTS THE STORY

.

MUM'S HEARBREAK WILL 'NEVER END' AFTER DAUGHTER TOOK HER OWN LIFE AFTER A ROW WITH PALS.

Karen Carter, from Burnley in Lancashire, says online bullying stole her daughter, Molly from her after she took her own life aged 20 following a row with friends over Parklife tickets.

Karen Carter, 48, has spoken out about the 'devastating effects of bullying on social media, which she says stole 20 year old Molly's life, which she says stole Molly from her. The aspiring hairdresser tragically died after a row with friends over Parklife tickets in the summer of 2017.
Molly had purchased a £70 ticket to the show, but her friends had taken it from her as they wanted to bring a different pal with them.
Karen, from Burnley in Lancashire, said it was the 'final straw' for her bubbly daughter, who often felt her friends were excluding her.
She says her daughter endured years of bullying, such as her friends leaving nasty comments on pictures online and going on holiday without her.
An inquest into her death last month recorded a verdict of 'Misadventure'- but Karen says this has left her feeling 'enraged' and empty; as many of her questions remain unanswered.
Now, in the hope of protecting other young people, Karen is urging people to be kinder to each other, and has spoken about how online abuse is 'impossible to escape'.

We have to be kinder to each other and realise that what we say and do can have an everlasting impact, she said…….

She was a bubbly, kind and friendly girl but she had some issues with her friends because they were excluding her a lot.

Online abuse is impossible to escape when I was younger the bullying would stop when you got home.

There were so many little things they would do, but they weren't little things to my Molly.

Parklife was the final straw for her, it all escalated from there.

Now I will never have her back. She's been stolen from me.

The loss of her daughter has left Karen, a former cleaner, unable to work and she now suffers with severe anxiety and PTSD.

My life will never be the same, something will always be missing, she said.

I want girls to know they can be themselves; they don't need to feel all that pressure you get from seeing comments online or nasty horrible things on social media.

Despite the arguments, Molly attended the festival in June 2017, but left after she'd become fearful her drink had been spiked. She rang her mum, saying someone had put something in her tea and that her friends were being 'nasty' to her.

After ten days under observations, at Burnley General Hospital she was sectioned and then transferred between mental health units in Blackburn, Bradford and eventually Blackpool over the space of two weeks. But a few weeks after being discharged, she was tragically found dead on 29 August 2017.

Karen, who is also a single mum to he daughter, 15 and her son, 26 says in the weeks before her death Molly was unrecognisable and looked like a 'Zombie'

She says her daughter, who had never been away from home, was 'never right' after being sectioned and that better support services for young people with mental illnesses are also needed.

'It's going to keep happening to young people until something is done about it.' she continued.

Molly always used to say that we've got to help people, she was so kind and thoughtful.

I miss her so much, she was my best friend, and we spent so much time together and spoke about everything. Not a day goes by that I don't think about her.

Samaritans (16 123) operate a 24-hour service.

Or if you'd prefer or to write it down - email the

Samaritans at jo@samaritans.org

People say it must get easier as time goes on, take it from me it doesn't. You have to learn to live with it. The mental health system need to drastically change, and I do believe at last it's beginning to learn more and do more for those who find themselves at rock bottom or feeling suicidal. I must put on record I had a great deal of help from Hazel Rowley, the hospital advocate, who taught me how to write a complaint letter and to do it in a correct manner when I had complained bitterly to the NHS about how badly Molly had been let down.

I'm so lucky to have met so many kind and helpful and caring people who have helped me enormously throughout the last few years and I'm totally grateful to all of them.

Finally, I must end with a quote in Molly's own words –

'Don't Lose Your Sparkle'

This seemed to me to be an appropriate title for this, my biography book. Molly was a very special daughter, a much loved granddaughter, a sister to her brother, Adam, her two sisters, Katie and Darcy and an Aunty to Harry and would have been had she lives to baby Ollie who will reach his 1st birthday any day soon.

I still miss Molly's sparkle every single day.

'Rest in peace, Molly. No-one can hurt you any more. Goodnight sweetheart.'

ACKNOWLEDGEMENTS

To Joyce Graham who has worked tirelessly as the ghost writer for this book. Also a big thank you to David, her husband, who has patiently supported her throughout the many hours of work needed.

All of my good friends: Gwyneth, Wendy, Sarah, Linda and family, there to get me through, I thank you all.

Big thanks for the kindness of all those students at Unity College, Burnley who attended and donated many useful items of night wear, day wear clothes, a massive amount of toiletries, games and puzzle books, for those who were locked up with absolutely nothing in the way of new clothes or decent night wear. Even a bar of soap was a luxury item, for them. The school had done them proud. The many items had been boxed up and presented to Mental Health Wards at the Burnley General Hospital and had been gratefully accepted,.

Another special day had been organised at Nelson & Colne College, where Molly had attended a hairdressing course and had made many friends there, all wanting to say their last goodbyes to Molly by holding a special 'Memorial Day for Molly'. A bench with a gold inscribed plaque in Molly's name had been placed in the peace garden for all to see. Any student wishing to sit and reflect, or to take a moment out to think of Molly, or simply find some kind of peace. I was truly touched by everyone who attended that day and thank you to everyone. Funds had been raised by the college and had been shared with MIND and the Samaritans Organisation. Thank you.

The Spiritual Church who also arranged for a night with a 'Medium', which also raised much needed fund monies for MIND.

Andrew's Butcher's in the Market Hall, again where Molly had been happy to serve and chat to all the customers, many of which have told me they missed her so much.

Finally, a big thank to all the lovely and thoughtful people who sent sympathy cards or came along to pay their last respects to Molly. It made our family feel the love on that sad occasion.

* In certain circumstances in this book, names have needed to be changed.

Printed in Great Britain
by Amazon